WHAT ARE **STUDENTS** SAYING ABOUT S·O·A·R™ Study Skills?

"Life is so much easier!"
- Holly Zabik, 9th grade student

"This (book) is very easy to understand. It is laid out neat... helped me a lot! Thank you for everything!"
- Adrienne Gurski, college freshman

"I am reading and reviewing chapters in my text books now. It's really easy and really helps me study for tests."
- Keith Schwartz, 6th grade student

"I liked how everything was grouped in categories and everything kind of set up the next step of SOAR™."
- Stephanie Craig, 11th grade student

"This book will influence people to become more focused on their objectives in school or any other situation."
- Christopher Mayburn, college senior

• • • • •

WHAT ARE **PARENTS** SAYING ABOUT S·O·A·R™ Study Skills?

"Everything is practical and easy to do. –Great tips! My son set up a SOAR™ Binder and it is working for him!"
- Janet Couture, elementary school parent

"Kurt is more focused about time management. The jar of priorities made a big impact on how he uses his time on a daily basis."
- Lachele Mangum, middle school parent

"My sons were good students to begin with, but they have used many SOAR™ strategies to make homework easier for them."
- Donna Bishop, elementary & middle school parent

• • • • •

WHAT ARE **TEACHERS** SAYING ABOUT S·O·A·R™ Study Skills?

"Excellent, useable information!"
- Lori Bolton, middle school study skills teacher

"Wonderful organizational ideas for students…prioritizing activity will be great to use with students. The writing tools will also be a significant help!"
- Nancy Anderson, high school resource teacher

"This is a great system! I would like to see my whole school use this. Would you be interested in training my colleagues?"
- Sarah Daniels, middle school teacher

Who Is Using SOAR®?

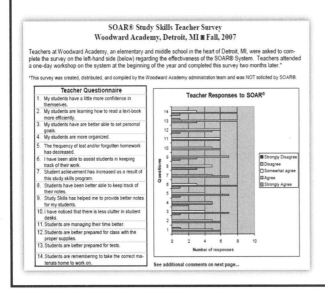

***SOAR® Study Skills* is the best-selling study skills book in the world!**

The *SOAR® Curriculum* is used in over 1000 schools world-wide… and growing daily! To see a more detailed list, visit: soarSS.com/SOARwu

Teachers Declare SOAR® 98.9% Effective in Improving Student Performance!

Teachers were asked to complete a survey regarding the effectiveness of the SOAR® System.

This survey was created, distributed, and compiled by a school administration team and was NOT solicited by SOAR®.

For more details, visit:
soarSS.com/SOARwu

Curriculum Supplements

for

- Middle School
- High School
- Learning Disabilities

Regardless if students are in 6th grade or seniors in college, the type of academic tasks they have to do are essentially the same. Therefore, the strategies in SOAR® are appropriate for students across a wide range of grade-levels and ability levels.

However, students of various ages and abilities have unique needs. We wanted to address these needs. But, we did not want to create multiple editions and "water down" our simple and solid strategies. So, we created another solution...

SOAR® Curriculum Supplements! This companion resource provides tips and strategies for students in middle school, high school, and students with learning disabilities.

Resources Include:

✓ **Pacing guidelines for instruction.**
(Including access to a video covering helpful pacing considerations.)

✓ **The best strategies in the *Multi-Media Teacher's Guide*** for middle school, high school, and students with learning disabilities.

✓ **Schedule templates:** Pick a schedule, plug in activities from SOAR®, and your lesson planning is done!

✓ **...and more!**

FREE

A $299 value...FREE with purchase of Curriculum from StudySkills.com!
(Minimum one *Multi-Media Teacher's Guide* & 30 books, or equivalent purchase.)

FREE Toolkits at StudySkills.com

The *Homework Rx*® and *Teacher Toolkits* compliment the systems and strategies presented in the *SOAR*® *Study Skills* book.

The Toolkits include a "Study Skills Scorecard" and our very popular guide:

25 Ways to Make Homework Easier...Tonight!

For Parents & Students

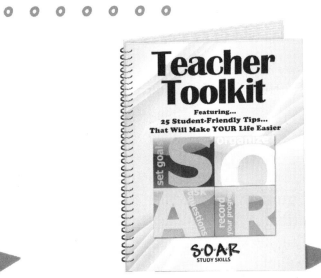

For Educators

To download your toolkit,
visit www.StudySkills.com.

Select the option that is most appropriate for you:

- Parents
- Students
- Educators

S·O·A·R™
STUDY SKILLS
A simple and efficient system for earning better grades in less time.

set goals
organize
ask questions
record your progress

Adding Wisdom Award
PARENT TO PARENT

Susan Kruger Woodcock, M.Ed.

Designed by Susan Kruger
Illustrations by Karl Mayry
Photographs by Dan Kruger & Cathy Scott Stoey
Graphic Illustrations by Joelle Geisler, Cathy Scott Stoey, & Susan Kruger
Cover Design by Cindy T. Chesney, Juice Box Design

Edited by Amanda Hayhoe & Cecelia Hissong
Reviewers: Lori Bolton, Adrienne Gurski, Amanda Hayhoe, Greg Kruger, Cecelia Hissong,
Cynthia Woodcock
Technical Consultant: Brian Woodcock

Internet: www.StudySkills.com
Email: info@StudySkills.com

Published by Grand Lighthouse Publishing, Grand Blanc, MI

Library of Congress Control Number: 2005935199
ISBN: 0-9774280-0-1
SAN: 257-6570

Printed in the United States of America

To the best parents a kid could ask for:

Mom—*who weathered countless homework storms before I learned all of this information.*

Dad– *who always encouraged me to "stick to my guns."*

And to the best husband a girl could ask for:

Brian—*a great teacher in the classroom...and in life.*

dedication

table of contents

acknowledgements

This book has been evolving since the day I started first grade and cried every night about my homework. (Sorry, Mom!) The greatest asset I have in writing this book is that I have been a student for a *very* long time and struggled in school for many years.

The puzzle did not come together for me until college when I had the opportunity to work with the people of *Self-Enhancement Services* at Western Michigan University. I thank them for being the first to provide me with a few workable strategies and the foundation for a much more successful school experience in college.

Thank you to Pam Romanelli and Sr. Elena Sabulusky for graciously passing my name along as a "study skills tutor" upon my college graduation and then inviting me to teach at my alma mater. When I first created the SOAR™ Study Skills Workshop, Sr. Cecilia Bondy opened her door and invited me to teach the program at Divine Child for many years.– I am very grateful to her for this opportunity!

Thank you to Tamara Moin and Dolly Moiseeff of the Oakland Press for carefully writing an article that captured the essence of my workshop and the positive impact it has on students. It was the overwhelming response I received from this article that influenced me to pursue study skills as a full-time career.

To all of the students who have attended the SOAR™ workshops over the years...I am grateful for your active participation, open minds, fabulous suggestions, and gracious feedback. Your energy and enthusiasm have inspired me to constantly improve and move SOAR™ to new heights.

Donna Bednarczyk...in a simple act of kindness, you gave my career wings. You are a constant source of encouragement and great "mommy mentor." To Luke...It was such an honor to be your teacher. Your mom says that my "Marky stories" are very similar to her "Luke stories." If that means that Mark grows up to be such a nice young man, I am a very luck mom.

Ginelle Barry…Thank you for so graciously helping us achieve some peace in our household. I also appreciate your talents in troubleshooting software and in editing photos and illustrations. You are another parenting role model for us and have become a good friend.

Cathy Scott Stoey...28 years ago, when we were sipping Pepsi® out of mugs and imitating coffee commercials at sleep-overs, did you ever think we would someday be turning your living room into a photo

studio to take pictures of school supplies? Since the first day that I asked you to help me with this project, you've been 100% on-board. I'm sorry it took me two years to complete it, but I have been grateful for your genuine support and encouragement along the way. You were exceptionally generous with your time and talents in the last few months of the project, taking/editing photos, and reassuring me that it would all turn out okay.–Thank you!

Karl Mayry...Your love of learning is infectious! I have learned so much random information from you and have had so many unique opportunities working with you. The amazing thing is, I've enjoyed it! I hope you pass your spirit for learning on to my son. Likewise, your incredible talent has helped this book come to life! Thank you for all of your drawings and for being so gracious with re-drawings. You have provided significant encouragement over the years in all of my career endeavors and have also been a good friend to our family. We are grateful to have you in our lives.

Cindy Chesney...They say you should never judge a book by its cover. In this case, however, I wouldn't mind if people do. The cover is beautiful! Your patience and assistance in preparing it, revising it, and getting it to the printer is very much appreciated.

Lori Bolton...thank you so much for bringing SOAR™ into your school and, in turn, sharing your suggestions for improvement. Your feedback has been very valuable and your encouragement is very much appreciated!

Adrienne Gurski...Brian & I are both very proud of all that you have accomplished and more importantly, for the person you are. You are very kind and have such a positive attitude towards life. I value your feedback, especially because you are right in the trenches...thank you for taking the time out of your busy schedule to help.

Not many people are lucky enough to have two brothers and a soon-to-be sister-in-law to call upon for such a variety of help. Dan, Greg, and Amanda...it's hard to tell each of you how much I appreciate your help with computer problems, websites, photo-taking, photo-editing, sharing business suggestions, and reviewing/editing this book. I am so grateful that I have each of your talents and skills to call upon and that you are all so grateful about assisting. Amanda, thank you for bailing me out of a tight situation...again!

Grandpa Willer...your stories of entrepreneurship and words of encouragement are very valuable. Thank you for having faith in me!

Mom and Dad Woodcock...This project would have taken me at least another five years to complete if it were not for your help. You have so graciously provided babysitting, assisted with household projects, made meals, maintained my computer, and done countless other little things that have allowed me to devote so much time to completing this project. Mom, thank you for reviewing the book and yes, your delicious home-made chocolate chip cookies were responsible for keeping this aspiring author happy and energized!

Mom & Dad Kruger...this book is dedicated to the two of you in recognition and appreciation for the great foundation you gave me. However, I must also thank you for all of your help in getting this book off the ground. You have given up hours of your time to take care of your grandson so that I could work (or in some cases, sleep). Meals, household projects, and editing are also on your list of credits. Mom, thank you for offering to do whatever it took in the last couple of weeks to help me make my deadline. Dad, thanks for being so excited for me!

Mark...you have a beautiful spirit and bring countless smiles to everyone you meet. The promise of being able to spend more time with you has been my biggest motivation to finish this book. I am excited and honored to be your mom.

Finally, to Brian...You have been so instrumental in every aspect of SOAR™, right from the beginning. You were good for the ideas when the program was first created and have never failed to bail me out of my creative slumps since. I could never thank you enough for all of the sacrifices you have made that have allowed me to pursue this project as well as all of the dinners, grocery trips, baby baths, commuting, and care-taking hours you have invested that allowed me to write. You are an amazing father and make being a mom very enjoyable. You keep this trip fun...I love you!

Would you like to earn better grades *and* have more time for fun?

If so, you have come to the right place! This book is for students in middle school through college who are looking for ways to improve their grades in less time. There are resources here for *every* student, regardless of whether you generally find school difficult or are simply looking for ways to maximize your study time. Strategies in this program are simple and student-friendly, allowing you to achieve a great balance between being a successful student and living a fun, enriched life.

If I can do it, *you* can do it!

SOAR™ Study Skills is a collection of tips and strategies I learned throughout my experiences as a student. In grade school and high school, I struggled to earn decent grades. I was the youngest person in my class and always felt like the whole world was smarter than I was. In college, however, I learned a few pointers that made studying much easier and helped me improve my grades instantly. In fact, after my first semester, I earned three As and one B+. Not only was this a far better GPA than I had ever earned before, it was actually easier to achieve than any of my previous school experiences. My success came down to learning *how to learn* more efficiently.

"How long will it take me to learn this program?"

Most of the techniques in this book can be used immediately. A few others take a bit of practice. You can put most pieces into regular use over the course of a month or a semester, depending on your level of commitment. You may also prefer to pick and choose just a few components out of the whole program. Your options are very flexible, which is exactly what makes the SOAR™ Study Skills Program so effective.

"How do I use this book?"

The book begins with a section called *How are you smart?* This chapter encourages you to explore your abilities and interests, recognizing the talents that you possess. While this section does not cover specific skills for studying, it is very important because doing well in school is much more than just knowing how to take good notes or study for a test. The road to success starts with an attitude of commitment and an aspiration to succeed. All human beings are born with the desire to achieve, yet some people lose sight of that goal if life experiences have taught them that success is out of their reach. In order to feel motivated in school, it helps to feel confident that you *do* have skills and talents, even if school-related tasks are not your strong points. I encourage you to take your time completing the quizzes and reviewing the information that best pertains to you.

The remaining sections of the book contain *core* strategies. There are literally hundreds of skills that you *could* learn, but my focus in creating this book was to cover the most important and fundamental skills necessary for school success, as discovered from my experience as a student and a teacher.   Those skills have been organized into four basic principles: **S**et goals, **O**rganize, **A**sk questions, and **R**ecord your progress. As you read the book, you may notice that some principles and strategies are repeated in a few places. This is not an oversight; it is to reinforce the fact that all four of the SOAR™ principles are interrelated and build upon one another. Once you have learned concepts for one step, you will have already learned half of the next step, and so on. The integrated nature of this program is what makes it so easy to learn and use. You are also welcome to read only the chapters of most interest to you at this time; you can start with only one section, or even one strategy. Once you see the difference one or two simple tips can make, you will want to learn more.

Students with Two Homes

If you call two places home, you will find helpful tips and suggestions throughout the book for managing your life from two locations.

"What have students said about SOAR™ Study Skills?"

I have taught hundreds of students from 5th grade through graduate school in my SOAR™ Study Skills Workshops and always request feedback from participants. Most students tell me that they like how easy it is to use this program. They are usually amazed that they notice a decrease in their workload and improvement in their scores so quickly. For many students, it is the first time that they have felt empowered to be successful in school. Parents also enjoy seeing their children take more initiative with their homework and feel happier about their performance in school. A few students have even said that it has changed their life! Actually, it is not *this program* that has changed their life, but their *awareness* that there are better, more efficient ways to do things.

Beyond SOAR™ Study Skills

After you have learned the SOAR™ system and practiced these core strategies for a while, you are likely to be interested in more specific study tools. For this reason, I will constantly be adding and updating my website, www.StudySkills.com, with additional, free resources that extend beyond the core strategies of SOAR™. I invite you to visit frequently and e-mail me with questions, comments, and stories about your school successes.

Welcome to the SOAR™ Study Skills Program! Whether your child struggles in school or you would simply like to see your child become more efficient with her school-work, this book will provide you with helpful strategies and insights designed to save time, reduce homework stress in the household, and empower your child to achieve success.

Is homework *too much* of a hassle?

As a teacher, I have worked with hundreds of parents striving to help their children realize success in school while also achieving peace at home. Throughout my experience teaching in the classroom, conferencing with parents, and visiting homes as a tutor, I discovered that the problems most students and families faced have very similar themes; many of which echoed my own experiences as a student. Do any of these comments sound familiar to you?

❏ **"I try to show him some better ways to do his homework, but he will not listen to me."**

❏ **"Her homework just takes over the family. We cannot get control of it and it causes many arguments."**

❏ **"He gets so frustrated and I do not know how to help him."**

❏ **"She has the potential, but…"**

❏ **"I never thought my child's homework could be so stressful!"**

If you can relate to any of these feelings, you are certainly not alone! Every day, I speak with parents who feel something must be wrong with them. After all, homework is just homework and should not create such a hassle, right? Ironically, homework represents so much more than a few daily assignments.

For most children/young adults, homework represents one of their first significant avenues of control as they grow towards independence. They often face a struggle between doing what they *want* to do and what they *should* do. Knowing that you place a significant value on homework, children of all ages often use it as a way of "taking control" from you. For most students, this is usually an innocent tug-of-war they may not even realize they are fighting. However, this understanding may provide some enlightenment about why homework can be such a struggle.

"How do I overcome the 'control' factor?"

The key is not to overcome the issue of control, but to work with it by empowering your child; give him a sense of control while establishing your expectations. To do this, give him specific choices. For example, instead of saying "You have to study for your science test." you can say, "You need to study for your science test this week. Would you like to study for 20 minutes on Monday & Wednesday or would you like to study for 10 minutes every night this week?" While that may sound very simple, it is a very effective example of how you can provide some choice (a.k.a. control) while still achieving a positive outcome.

Using SOAR™ Study Skills with Your Child

The best way to ensure cooperation from your child is to read this book together. Read one chapter at a time and discuss the content. As you read, ask your child why he thinks a specific strategy would work and how he thinks he might benefit from giving it a try. Empower him for success by asking for his opinion about each strategy. During the *Set goals* section, be sure to let him set his own goals and respect his privacy if he would prefer not to show them to you. (He may be reluctant to share his goals if he is afraid he might not achieve them or that you will punish him for not reaching them.)

If you suspect that your child might be resistant to trying some of these strategies, read the book first and determine some "either/or" options you can offer him to give him a sense of control. To begin, you may want to focus only on the area that you feel is the biggest problem for your child and only do one or two strategies before trying others. Many of the strategies are also ideal for adults, so start by modeling the use of a few yourself.

"How long will it take my child to learn this program?"

This book can be read all at one time or chapter by chapter, therefore the pacing will be up to you and your child. Never rush your child through several strategies at one time; she will only become frustrated and the entire process will backfire. However, with a positive partnership between the two of you, it is possible to implement the entire program in 4-6 weeks. It will probably take a full semester (4 to 5 months) before the strategies become part of a *natural* routine.

Features of the SOAR™ Skills Program

The first section, *How are you smart?,* encourages your student to ex-
amine his talents and evaluate his strengths. Quite often, difficulty in
school leads people of all ages to believe that they lack intelligence.
How Are You Smart? is designed to help your child discover that he *is* a
very smart individual, regardless of the grades he has earned in the past.
This section is also good for you to review, especially if you are frustrated by his performance in school; it serves as a reminder to notice
and appreciate the positive gifts that your child possesses.

All of the strategies in the remaining four sections share one common
thread… they are simple to use. This simplicity is what sets the
SOAR™ Study Skills Program apart from other similar resources.
Each component selected or created for this program is designed to not
only help raise grades, but to ultimately save time and minimize has-
sles. Each of the four SOAR™ principles: **S**et goals, **O**rganize, **A**sk
questions, and **R**ecord your progress sets the stage for the subsequent
section and reinforces strategies from the previous sections. The interrelated nature of this program is the key to its success because the steps
are comprehensive and easy to remember.

Thank you for making the commitment to help your child discover success in school. I sincerely appreciate the opportunity to share my
knowledge and experiences with you and I hope this program provides
you with many helpful tools. I will continuously update my website,
www.StudySkills.com, with additional tools and free resources, so
please visit often. You are also invited to e-mail me with questions,
comments, and stories about your experience with the SOAR™ Study
Skills Program.

Welcome to SOAR™ Study Skills! Whether you would like to integrate study skills into your established curriculum or teach a specific study skills course, this book has plenty of resources to meet your needs.

A One-of-a-Kind Study Skills Resource

The SOAR™ Study Skills Program is unlike other study skills resources that simply list a variety of study techniques. Those formats are often difficult for students to comprehend, or determine when to use particular procedures. Instead, the SOAR™ Program consists of specific, core strategies that have been broken down into four principles: **S**et goals, **O**rganize, **A**sk questions, **R**ecord your progress. These core strategies cover the most fundamental skills for school success and interrelate with one another, making it easy for students to learn and use them immediately. The techniques within each section lay a foundation for the following section and conversely, reinforce strategies from previous sections. SOAR™ is much more than a list; it is truly a comprehensive program.

Using SOAR™ Study Skills in the Classroom

In a classroom setting of any kind, students will achieve the greatest rate of success if they can apply each method directly to their school work. For example, if you are integrating these techniques into your science instruction, then it is best to teach, model, and practice each technique with your science content, homework, text books, tests, etc. If you teach a separate study skills class, then students must be encouraged to use homework and text books from other classes as they learn the program. Students will not remember and/or apply this information as effectively if they practice the strategies with generic assignments.

There are very few supplies needed to execute this program, but it would certainly be beneficial for all students to have the basic binder supplies and a planner. Some companies sell custom designed planners with a school's logo, annual calendar, and other pertinent information printed inside (links for reputable companies can be found on our website). If you are not able to purchase planners, you can reproduce the weekly planner page in the Appendix of this book. The SOAR™ Binder System is an essential piece of this program. With the volume and tax discounts available to schools, the supplies needed for the binder should be very inexpensive.

The SOAR™ Study Skills Program can provide exponential results if

an entire school community assimilates some or all of the strategies across the curriculum areas. The system is not time-consuming to teach when it is used in conjunction with lessons and assignments that teachers would normally administer and is very effective when it is reinforced across several different classes. In-services are available for schools interested in adopting the program. Log onto to www.StudySkills.com for more information.

"How much time will it take to teach this material?"

When integrating these skills into content-area classes, the additional time needed for instruction will be minimal because the strategies become part of the lessons and assignments. For classes that focus exclusively on study skills, there is enough material for approximately five to six weeks of instruction with application. Afterwards, time is best spent customizing instruction for small groups of students and focusing on the specific needs of students. At the time of this printing, I am in the process of developing assessment rubrics, extension lessons, and grouping guides for classroom use. Please check our website, www.StudySkills.com, for updates, as they will be posted frequently.

SOAR™ing with Your Students

Finally, as you learn and teach the program, you are likely to discover modifications and enhancements that work well with your students. I invite you to share your feedback. Please e-mail me (via the website) with questions, comments, and suggestions for improvement. I am also eager to know if you have a need for additional study skills materials to help you in the classroom. Your responses will allow me to keep the program fresh and up-to-date so that I may continue to reach students for years to come.

Genius in Sheep's Clothing

I have many friends, relatives, and students who have been diagnosed with Attention Deficit Hyperactivity Disorder and they all have one thing in common (other than their diagnosis)…They are brilliant! Each and every one of them have highly unique gifts for creating, designing, and building things, telling stories, socializing with others, developing creative solutions…the list goes on. People with ADD/ADHD are usually very intelligent. Ironically, it is this trait that causes them so much trouble; they are interested in such a variety of things, they have a hard time narrowing their focus.

Unfortunately, the school environment often makes it difficult for a student with ADD/ADHD (herein referred to as ADHD) to achieve success. While most educators always strive to improve instruction for all students, the very nature of a school setting presents challenges to the student with ADHD. However, these hurdles are not impossible to overcome!

Rising to the Challenge

Regardless of what your academic experience has been in the past, there are strategies you can learn that will make school much easier for you and allow you to earn better grades. The key is to learn a few strategies well and practice them until they become second-nature for you. Like everyone, you will have times when you are knocked off course a bit, but once you develop a habit, it will be easier to get back on track quickly.

The strategies in SOAR™ Study Skills have all been selected or created because they are simple and student-friendly. They all interrelate with each other, making it easy to learn and remember them. They provide you with concrete guidelines and routines that will turn some of the most difficult tasks into a piece of cake!

Important Considerations

Before exploring specific strategies, it is important to consider the following things about ADHD:

ADHD is a medical condition. It can only be diagnosed by a qualified medical professional. If you have not been diagnosed, but suspect you may have ADHD, contact a physician as soon as possible. One of

guidelines for students with ADD/ADHD

the best ways to deal with ADHD is to simply *know* that you have it and understand what it is.

Become educated about ADHD. The more you know about the condition, the more empowered you will be to deal with it. You will have a greater appreciation for your strengths and a better understanding of your weaknesses. With this information, you will learn specific tactics to accentuate your positive points and triumph over your short-comings.

If prescribed, take your medication. Certainly, medicine is not the only solution, but it can be a very helpful one if you and your doctor have determined it is appropriate for you. Often, people are afraid that taking medication for ADHD will change their personality. –It shouldn't! Every person I know who has been medically treated for ADHD finds that they can see life a bit more clearly. As one adult relative said, "For the first time in my life, I do not feel like I am living in a tunnel!"

Enlist the help of a coach. A coach can be a trusted friend, relative, or even a professional. The coach's job is to help you stay on track and achieve your goals. Some people find that a coach is very helpful for a short time (6 months-year) as they learn and develop new habits, but others find that a coach is a helpful life-long tool. Obviously, this person should be trustworthy and give you lots of positive encouragement as well as constructive criticism. You will need to be confident that he values your talents and strengths when he has to tell you something that might be hard to hear.

Create structure. The ADHD mind has a difficult time *creating* structure, which is why outside structure is so important. This reason is why SOAR™ Study Skills is so helpful; the entire book provides strategies to help you create structure in your life.

The strategies in SOAR™ Study Skills are great tools for developing the structure that is so beneficial for students with ADHD.

Key Strategies for School Success

A few helpful strategies for creating structure and enhancing your school performance are listed below. Many of these will be repeated later in the book, but they are presented here as examples of **key concepts** for dealing with ADHD.

Use the SOAR™ Binder System. The binder (described on page 41) will streamline all of your papers and notebooks into one location, minimizing the amount of "stuff" that you have to organize.

Keep your binder and planner easily accessible throughout the day. Chances are good that you like to do things quickly, so keep your binder and planner on your desk to make it easy for you to use these tools.

Stay healthy and active. While staying fit is healthy for everyone, it is especially important for people that experience hyperactivity. Participating in structured sports not only channels all of your extra energy in a positive way, it helps develop good self-discipline skills.

When reading your notes, read them out loud AND walk around, do some jumping jacks...anything active. Moving and talking will help channel your focus in more positive way, which will increase your ability to learn and remember new information.

Break homework up into smaller chunks. To keep homework from overwhelming you, set a timer and plan your homework in 20-30 minute intervals. Then, challenge yourself to finish a certain amount of work before the timer goes off. If you are feeling anxious about the amount of work you have to do, place a piece of paper over your assignment so that you can only see one row of problems at a time.

Use a keyboard. Often, people with ADHD are not very efficient writers. A keyboard often serves as a more effective alternative for writing assignments because thoughts from your brain can be recorded much more quickly with a keypad.

Think with a pen in hand. People with ADHD often have to be doing something to help them focus. Draw pictures, graphs, or symbols that illustrate important concepts as you listen to your teacher in class.

These are just a few of many potential methods for making the detour around ADHD and achieving success in school. Good luck!

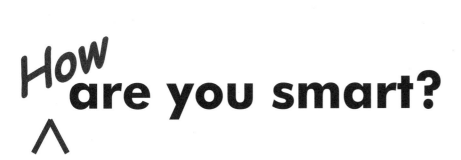

How **are you smart?**
∧

chapter 1

chapter 1

Many Types of Intelligence

section

1

chapter 1
Many Types of Intelligence

There are many children and adults who go through life feeling *dumb, stupid,* or simply *not smart* typically because of struggles they have had in school. Getting a good education is extremely important, but performance in school is not the only measure of a person's intelligence. You probably know many adults who did not get *good* grades in school, yet are talented artists, businesspeople, tradesmen, etc. Fortunately, many teachers are beginning to realize that intelligence is measured by more than students' performance on tests and written assignments.

Over the last 20 years, Dr. Howard Gardner[1], Professor of Education at Harvard University, has been doing research on intelligence. He suggests that there are at least eight different types of human intelligence:

Body Smart
(Bodily Intelligence)

Picture/Visual Smart
(Spatial Intelligence)

Music Smart
(Musical Intelligence)

People Smart
(Interpersonal Intelligence)

Word Smart
(Linguistic Intelligence)

Self Smart
(Intrapersonal Intelligence)

Number/Reasoning Smart
(Logical-Mathematical Intelligence)

Nature Smart
(Naturalist Intelligence)

Why are these types of intelligences important?

Schools traditionally measure students' abilities in only two intelligences: Number/Reasoning and Word Smarts. While these intelligences are important, they are not the only proof of one's aptitude. For example, I once had a student who struggled with reading, writing, and math assignments (traditional school work). However, he demonstrated an amazing ability to construct objects and machines from scrap materials. He could draw complex diagrams and figure out, with very little effort, how anything mechanical worked. Many teachers viewed him as a "slow learner" when in fact he simply struggled in two areas of intelligence (Word Smart and Number/Reasoning Smart). This student had the potential to become, among other things, a very successful mechanic or industrial engineer.

> *Before any of the content in the rest of this book can be helpful for you, you must believe in yourself, have confidence that you do have talents, and trust that you can accomplish anything you set your mind to.*

Too many people (students *and* adults) struggle because they lack confidence in their abilities. They often think, "I may be a good artist, but I'm not smart," or "I may be good at repairing things, but I'm not intelligent!" It is unfortunate that a great actor or comedian may not view his talent as a form of intelligence… Each and every person is smart! Even a person who has a mental disability is likely to be gifted in some areas (interpersonal intelligence, for example).

Before any of the content in the rest of the book can be helpful for you, you must believe in yourself, have confidence that you *do* have talents, and trust that you can accomplish anything you set your mind to. If you have experienced problems in school, chances are that you simply have not been given the tools to break down the wall. Sections two through five of this book provides those tools. In the meantime, the following two pages encourage you to identify some of your natural strengths and the various ways that you are intelligent (you can have strengths in many different areas of intelligence). **Everybody has their own special talents…Find yours and develop confidence in your own** *smart self.*

---

[1] Gardner, Howard. <u>Intelligences Reframed: Multiple Intelligences for the 21st Century</u>. New York: Basic Books, 1999.

How are you smart?

Do you enjoy, or feel talented in, any of the following activities?
Take this quiz and check all that apply:

Check		
	Artistic projects such as drawing, painting, crafting, etc.	
	Helping/caring for other people (e.g. children, senior citizens)	
	Singing, composing, or playing a musical instrument	
	Completing math or logic problems	
	Journaling, meditating, or reflecting on thoughts and feelings	
	Building, creating, or fixing things	
	Working or playing outdoors	
	Speaking in front of large groups	
	Sports, dance, or performing arts	
	Day-dreaming or picturing possibilities for yourself	
	Figuring out how things work	
	Decorating or arranging rooms	
	Listening to music to adjust your mood	
	Communicating with others or working effectively with a team	
	Setting and accomplishing goals for yourself	
	Working with animals and/or plants	
	Conversing with others, telling jokes, or stories	
	Humming or whistling while you work on other tasks	
	Classifying or organizing objects	
	Hunting, camping, or hiking	
	Completing tasks on the computer or playing video games	
	Making people feel comfortable	
	Reading maps	
	Learning or speaking foreign languages	

How are you smart? quiz format is adapted from SuperCamp®.

Would you describe yourself as:

Check		
	Athletic	
	Being an enthusiastic reader or writer	
	A problem solver	
	Musical	
	Visual	
	Friendly or patient with others	
	"Nature lover"	
	Spiritual, thoughtful, or insightful	
	Good with numbers	
	Having a sense of rhythm	
	Active	
	Sensitive to sounds, tones, or accents	
	Creative	
	Self-disciplined or independent	
	Good "referee" with your friends and/or family	
	"Animal lover"	

Scoring

To identify your strongest "smarts," match the icon at the end of each checked item (from both pages) with the corresponding columns below. Create a bar graph of your results by shading in one box for every quiz item that has been checked, beginning at the bottom of each column.

How are you smart?

Math	Visual	Word	Music	People	Self	Body	Nature

You may have found that you have interests and strengths in several different areas. Hopefully you are beginning to get a sense of what each area of intelligence really means. Listed below are further descriptions:

Body Smart (Bodily-Kinesthetic Intelligence)

People who are gifted in this area generally enjoy sports, dance, or other areas of physical fitness. They are often referred to as "active" because they love to move! They learn best through movement and hands-on activities.

People in careers that enhance this intelligence include:

Craftspeople, physical/occupational therapists, surgeons, inventors, professional athletes, actors, farmers, dancers

Music Smart (Musical/Rhythmic Intelligence)

You do not have to be a gifted singer, composer, or instrument player to have talent in this area. You may enjoy music or have a strong sense of rhythm. You may learn best through songs, patterns, rhythms, and other forms of musical expression, or find yourself frequently tapping and/or dancing to music.

People in careers that enhance this intelligence include:

Composers, song-writers, sound technicians, disc jockeys, instrument makers, music teachers, band directors

Word Smart (Linguistic Intelligence)

Word Smart people are often good at reading, writing, speaking, or a combination of the three. They may enjoy reading and written expression, find they are good at telling jokes and stories, or speaking in front of others. They may also have an interest in foreign languages. Some people may be very gifted in one area of Linguistic Intelligence, such as conversation skills, but may struggle with another area, such as writing.

People in careers that enhance this intelligence include:

Salespeople, journalists/writers, editors, librarians, therapists, speech therapists, lawyers, interpreters

Number/Reasoning Smart (Logical/Mathematical Intelligence)

People with talents in this area are generally good math students. They are good at solving problems and puzzles with numbers or logic. Some are excellent at computing numbers in their head, estimating, or making conversions (e.g. in recipes). They may enjoy organizing, budgeting, or creating patterns.

People in careers that enhance this intelligence include:

Engineers, computer technicians/programmers, accountants, mathematicians, researchers, statisticians, financial analysts, professional organizers, physicians

Picture/Visual Smart (Spatial Intelligence)

While you don't have to be gifted in Picture Smarts to be called "creative," this is the term that is most often associated with individuals talented in Spatial Intelligence. People with strengths in this area are likely good at following or creating maps, noticing patterns, or assembling projects and puzzles. "Artistic" or "crafty" people are also gifted in Spatial Intelligence.

People in careers that enhance this intelligence include:

Graphic artists, interior designers, architects, engineers, photographers, videographers, inventors, drafters, builders, surveyors, urban planners

People Smart (Interpersonal Intelligence)

People Smart refers to the skills required to develop relationships with others. Individuals gifted in this intelligence usually work very well on teams and are skilled at making people feel comfortable in their presence. They usually enjoy helping others and may be good at resolving conflicts among family members and friends. Some People Smart individuals are very social and outgoing, while others may be reserved and shy. Either way, they are usually regarded as "nice" people.

People in careers that enhance this intelligence include:

Teachers, nurses, physicians, medical assistants, politicians, sales people, counselors/psychologists, mediators, consultants, business administrators (management), human resources

Self Smart (Intrapersonal Intelligence)

How well do you know yourself? If you are a reflective thinker, have a clear concept of your values and beliefs, or have a sense of spirituality or greater purpose, then you are probably very Self Smart. Because Self Smart individuals have a strong concept of what they want in life, they are likely to be very focused, self-disciplined, and independent. This intelligence usually develops with age and maturity.

People in careers that enhance this Intelligence include:

Writers, entrepreneurs/self-employed, spiritual leaders, counselors/ therapists, leaders, researchers

Nature Smart (Naturalist Intelligence)

"Nature Smart" people are inclined to be outdoors. They usually have a strong appreciation for the environment and respect for the beauty of nature. They typically are interested in plants, animals, or other natural resources and tend to choose activities such as hiking, camping, hunting, star gazing, swimming, scuba diving, etc. as hobbies.

People in careers that enhance this Intelligence include:

Meteorologists, park rangers, photo journalists, biologists, botanists, zoologists, veterinarians, anthropologists, sailors, astronomers

Intelligences & Study Skills

Hopefully, you learned a little more about yourself after reading this section. You have to recognize and feel good about your talents in order to be motivated in school and in life. This internal motivation will help make the strategies in this program easier for you to implement.

As you begin to read about the SOAR™ Study Skills program, keep in mind that it is designed to help you organize your time and materials, as well as to increase your effectiveness on traditional school assignments. However, the principles addressed in the program can be applied well beyond your school years and into your professional work life.

How are you smart?

-Summary-

1 **Everyone is intelligent!** There are at least eight different domains of intelligence, but school work typically assesses only two types of intelligence, Math and Word Smarts.

2 **There are careers suited for every type of intelligence.** Even if Math and Word Smarts are not your top talents, you will be able to find a career that fits your natural gifts. In the meantime, try to sign up for elective classes and extra-curricular activities that match your natural aptitudes.

3 **In order to be motivated in school and in life, you must recognize your intelligences and believe in your abilities.** When you feel good about yourself, you will soon discover that you can accomplish anything you set your mind to.

4 **Regardless of what your strongest intelligences are, it is important to get the best education you can get.** This book offers tips and strategies to help <u>all</u> students make school and homework easier.

Set goals

section

2

Set goals

Check all statements below that apply to you:

_____ Do you feel that your homework takes longer than it should?

_____ Would you like to earn better grades while still having time for extra-curricular activities and socializing?

_____ Do you ever forget what you have for homework?

_____ Do you ever forget certain books, notebooks, or folders at school that you need for homework?

_____ Are you tired of being nagged by your parents about homework and studying?

You will find solutions to these problems, and much more, in the following section.

The reason most people never reach their goals is that they don't define them, or ever seriously consider them as believable or achievable.

Winners *can tell you where they are going, what they plan to do along the way, and who will be sharing the adventure with them.*

- Denis Watley

In order to achieve better grades and use your time more efficiently, you must set goals for yourself. The process of setting a goal is much like planning a trip; you must have a destination and a plan for how you will get there. The process of setting goals helps you focus on your desired achievements, minimize distractions, and identify time-saving steps along your way.

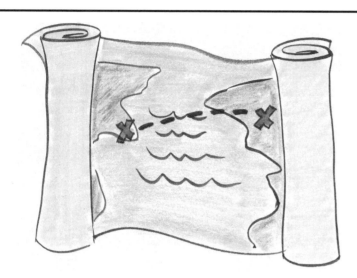

The process of setting a goal is much like planning a trip; you must have a destination and a plan for how you will get there.

The "map" in this program will take you through an in-depth journey for setting and achieving goals. As you complete the steps in this book, you will discover the important parts of identifying and reaching your goals. However, you will probably not need to be as thorough when setting goals in the future. After going through this process once, you will have the awareness and skills necessary to reach for, and achieve, anything you want!

□　□　□　□　□

The *Set goals* section of this book is broken down into the following three steps:

Establish your priorities.
Identify your goals.
Schedule time to take action.

These steps are highlighted at the beginning of each chapter to remind you of how each of the components fit together.

chapter 2

Establish Your Priorities
Identify Your Goals
Schedule Time to Take Action

In order to *Set goals*, you must first clearly understand your priorities, the things that are most important to you. Happy, successful people will tell you that the their happiness is achieved by making decisions according to their priorities, which minimizes time and energy wasters in their lives. Identifying your most important priorities will help you determine your goals and also help you make important decisions about how you spend your time.

Making Time for School *and* Fun Stuff

While school is very important and should be a top priority, "fun stuff" is just as important. **The key is to find a good balance.** In this section, you will learn strategies for balancing everything you *have* to do with everything you *want* to do!

The pictures on the next page illustrate an important concept about prioritizing your time. Can you figure out what that concept is?

What can a jar teach us about prioritizing?

1 This jar represents one day—24 hours—no more, no less.

2 As you know, a day fills up fast. So does the jar.

-Is this jar full?-

There is no more room for rocks, but....

3 ...there is plenty of room for pebbles.

-Is it full yet?-

There is not much more room for pebbles, but....

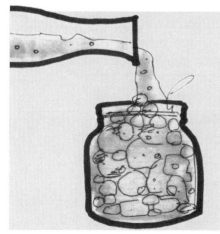

4 ...there is, of course, room for a lot of water.

-Is it full now?-

It certainly is!

Rock, pebble, and water analogy adapted from: Covey, Sean. The 7 Habits of Highly Effective Teens. Salt Lake City, UT: Franklin Covey Co., 2000.

..."So, what's the point?"

...That we have a lot of 'big' things and 'little' things to do in one day.

...That we can fit a lot into one day!

Both of these observations are partially correct, but there is more to it.

The significance of the rock, pebble, and water activity is the *order* in which the items were added to the jar. If we had started by filling the jar with pebbles, we wouldn't have had any room for rocks.

The jar is like your time; just as the big rocks automatically made room for pebbles and water, you can automatically make room for "fun stuff" when you take care of your big priorities first.

"How can this help me manage my time?"

When you have a clear sense of what your top priorities are (your big rocks) and you give your attention to those tasks first, you will be amazed at how much time you automatically have for other, more enjoyable things. For example, if you come home from school and start your homework within a half-hour of being home, you are taking care of a "rock" priority first. By tackling your homework right

As sure as a law of physics,
homework that is started at 4:00 p.m.
will get done faster than homework that
is started at 8:00 p.m.

away, you are more fresh and more efficient than if you wait until later in the evening. You will also be more likely to stay focused and get your work done quickly because the promise of a few, home-work free hours is extremely motivating.

Obviously, when your homework is done faster, you'll have more free time.

But that's not all...

When your homework is done, your free time is MUCH more enjoyable than when you take your free time first and have the burden of homework hanging over your head all evening.

"How do I determine what my priorities are?"

On the next two pages, you will be asked to think about all of the ways you currently spend your time and how you would like to spend your time. Then, you will have the opportunity to sort each item into a rock, pebble, or water category. A description of each category is below.

Rock Priorities

Your rock priorities are the things you have to do. You have to go to school, do homework, help around the house, sleep, etc. These things usually have significant consequences if not done. Such consequences include, but are not limited to: getting bad grades, flunking, being grounded, and being too tired to function properly.

Pebble Priorities

Pebble priorities are the things that you really enjoy and *want* to spend more time doing. Some examples may include sports, band, other extra-curricular activities at school, a part-time job, a hobby, and more time to socialize with friends. Your pebble priorities are the "spice" in your life...the things that provide you with a satisfying sense of enjoyment. These priorities are "smaller" because they do not have as many consequences if not done, **however smaller does not mean less significant.** You need to have a smart balance between rock and pebble priorities to lead a healthy life and maintain motivation for your rock priorities.

Water Priorities

Water priorities are "If I get to them, great. If not, oh well!" priorities. These are the little things that you enjoy doing, but do not necessarily need to schedule into your day, such as playing video games, playing with your dog, watching TV, etc. It can sometimes be hard to distinguish between pebble and water priorities. If you are undecided about which category something belongs in, your indecision is a good sign that the task belongs in the 'water' category. Water priorities will have less significance than either rock or pebble priorities if not done.

How do you spend your time?

In the chart below, make a list of everything you <u>like</u> to do and <u>have</u> to do with your time. Include school, homework, free-time activities, chores, and religious events (e.g. attending church/synagogue, if applicable). Also record how much time you spend on each activity per week. Finally, make a list of things you would like to have more time to do.

How I Spend My Time:	Amount of Time per Week:

Things I Would Like to Have More Time to Do:	Desired Amount of Time per Week:

What are your priorities?

Use the "How do your spend your time?" list from the previous page to determine your rock, pebble, and water priorities.

My "Rock" Priorities are:

(Things you <u>have</u> to do such as school, homework, chores, family responsibilities, church/synagogue, etc.)

_____   _____
_____   _____
_____   _____
_____   _____
_____   _____

My "Pebble" Priorities are:

(Things you <u>enjoy</u> doing and for which you want to make time such as sports, friends, specific TV shows, etc.)

_____   _____
_____   _____
_____   _____
_____   _____

My "Water" Priorities are:

(Things you enjoy doing but do not feel the need to schedule, such as watching general TV shows, instant messaging, etc.)

_____   _____
_____   _____
_____   _____
_____   _____

chapter 3

Establish Your Priorities
Identify Your Goals
Schedule Time to Take Action

Now that you have analyzed your priorities, you can determine what you would like to accomplish. Maybe you would like to get better grades, have more free time, or make the varsity basketball team. Anything is possible if you make plans for what you want to accomplish by setting goals.

Helpful Hint

One of your priorities should benefit your health. Examples include goals related to sports/physical fitness, healthy eating, and getting enough sleep.

Step 1: Identify Your Top Priorities

Choose three significant priorities from the previous page and record them below. To maintain a healthy balance in your life, make sure at least one priority is for school or homework (which should be listed as a rock priority), and one priority is from your pebble category. The third priority can be from either the rock or pebble category.

priority 1   Rock Priority—School/Homework

_____

priority 2   Pebble Priority

_____

priority 3   Rock or Pebble Priority

_____

Step 2: Turn Your Priorities Into Goals

Turn your priorities from the previous page into goals by answering the following questions.

priority 1

Rock Priority—School/Homework

How do you want to improve in this aspect of your life? What would you like to accomplish?

_____

_____

_____

_____

priority 2

Pebble Priority

How do you want to improve in this aspect of your life? What would you like to accomplish?

_____

_____

_____

_____

priority 3

Rock or Pebble Priority

How do you want to improve in this aspect of your life? What would you like to accomplish?

_____

_____

_____

_____

Step 3: Create a Plan for Achieving Your Goals

Most significant goals cannot be accomplished in one day; they usually require many steps over a long period of time. Therefore, you have to do more than just create goals, you have to create a plan for achieving them by breaking them down into smaller, manageable steps.

On page 24, you will make a specific list of all the things you need to do in order to achieve the three goals you just described. Follow the guidelines below for creating an effective plan for achieving your objectives.

1 **Write down each goal at the top of the three ladders on page 24.**

Imagine your goals are at the top of a ladder…and each rung of the ladder is a step towards your goal.

Reaching for a goal is like climbing a ladder… you go one step at a time.

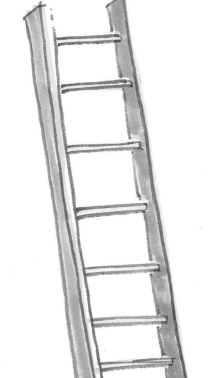

2 **Think about every little step you will need to accomplish in order to reach your goal. List the steps in the sections under each specific goal.**

Be specific in describing each action; you must be able to physically do each task. You must be able to close your eyes and actually visualize yourself doing the task. For example, you cannot see yourself getting good grades, but you can see yourself reviewing your notes every night for 20 minutes.

3 **See the sample list of goals on page 23 to help you identify appropriate, specific actions.**

Note that one of the lists includes more steps than others. You will find some goals require many steps and others require just a few.

Also, note that some goals will rely on other goals. For example, in order to accomplish the third goal on page 23, this person will rely on steps from the first goal.

GOAL

Raise every grade by one letter this quarter.

Action
Plan my week on Sundays.

(See Chapter 7.)

Action
Use my planner every day.

Action
Spend 10 min. at the end of each day reviewing notes.

Action
Keep all of my papers organized in a SOAR™ Binder.
(See Chapter 5.)

Action
Go to math tutoring during lunch once a week.

Action
Turn in all of my homework.

Action

GOAL

Stay in shape so I can make the varsity basketball team.

Action
Shoot hoops for 20 minutes, 3 days a week.

Action
Join a recreational league over the summer.

Action
Run for 20 minutes, 2-3 times per week.

Action
Lift weights when coach opens up the gym after school.

Action

Action

Action

GOAL

Spend more time friends, while getting good grades.

Action
Do everything listed under the first goal.

Action
Do as much homework in school as possible.

Action
Do h.w. as soon as I get home so I have more time at night.

Action
Ask my parents for rides (or the car) at the beg. of the week or ASAP.

Action

Action

Action

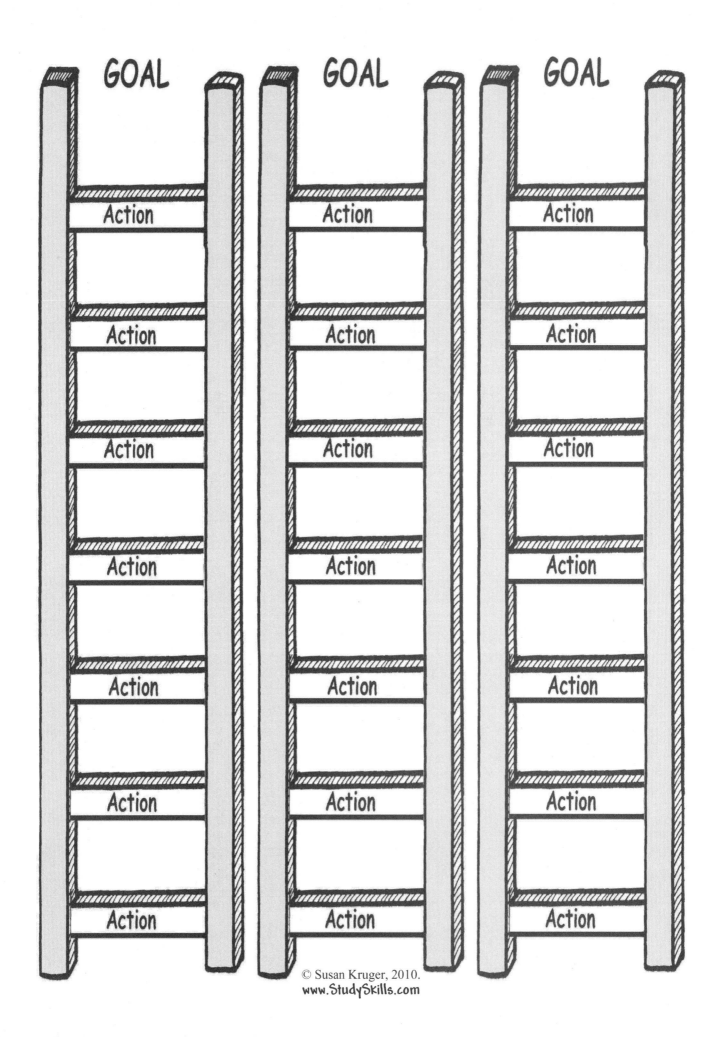

GOAL

GOAL

GOAL

Action

Action

Action

Action

Action

Action

Action

Action

Action

Action

Action

Action

Action

Action

Action

Action

Action

Action

Action

Action

Action

chapter 4

Establish Your Priorities
Identify Your Goals
Schedule Time to Take Action

Now that you have identified a few major goals and the action needed to achieve those goals, you need to make a plan for reaching them.

The Time Tool

The best tool for scheduling time and managing responsibilities is an academic planner. The task of juggling school, homework, family,

A planner is a living tool that serves as your base for evaluating priorities, keeping track of responsibilities, and making decisions about how to spend your time.

and social responsibilities is an on-going process that constantly needs to be planned, updated, and improved. A planner is a living tool that serves as your base for evaluating priorities, keeping track of responsibilities, and making decisions about how to spend your time.

If you think planners do not work for you, then you probably:

> **Planners don't work for me!**

a) have not been using the right planner
b) have not used a planner correctly
c) have not taken the time to develop the habit of using a planner
d) some or all of the above

☐ ☐ ☐ ☐ ☐

> **I do just fine without a planner!**

Have you ever forgotten one assignment or book for homework? Forgotten about a test? If so, you are not doing as well as you could be.

Planners work for everyone...

A planner is a great tool for people who tend to be a bit anxious, because it helps them keep track of what needs to be done and gives them a sense of control.

For people who tend to be more "last-minute," planners help them do exactly what they are probably not comfortable doing…planning ahead to avoid last-minute headaches.

A planner is absolutely necessary to achieve balance with your priorities and maximize your time.

Using a Planner

On the following timeline, you will learn strategies for using a planner effectively throughout different parts of the school day and week.

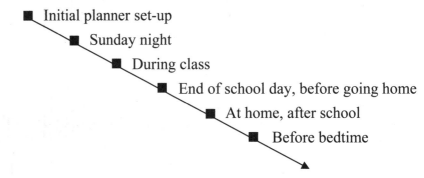

- Initial planner set-up
- Sunday night
- During class
- End of school day, before going home
- At home, after school
- Before bedtime

If you are not accustomed to using a planner, it may take two to three weeks before you remember to use it regularly, but do not give up! It takes a few pages to describe some simple tips, but it will not take very long to make this tool work for you!

Initial Planner Set-Up

Instantly open your planner to the current page with a binder clip. You are much more likely to use your planner if you do not have to flip through dozens of pages every time you need to write something down. (Paper clips do not work well because they slip off very easily.)

Write the phone numbers of responsible classmates from each of your classes in the back of your planner, in case you ever have questions about homework. Do not use e-mail or instant messaging for this purpose. E-mail is not reliable because you have to wait for friends to check it and instant messaging provides a strong temptation to get sucked into the computer. Save e-mail/instant messaging for after your homework is complete, when you can enjoy it without worrying about homework.

Sunday Night

Spend ten minutes on Sundays preparing for the week. Pull out your planner and write down your goals for the week, sports practices, project due dates, test dates, work schedules, etc. Highlight test or project due dates and then consider, "What do I have the night before?" If you have a basketball game the night before a big test, then you need to plan on spending extra time studying two nights before the test.

Do you ever feel like your parents nag you too much? Would you like them to stop?

Involve them when you plan your week. Ask your parents what their schedules are for the week and if they have anything planned for you, such as a doctor appointment or birthday dinner for your great-aunt. Let them know what you have going on, as well.

Parents "nag" because they want to be sure you are getting your homework done, that you are getting good grades, etc. They want what is best for you! If **you** take the initiative to tell your parents what is going on and communicate your plans for completing homework, you will be letting your parents know that you have things under control. When parents know you have things under control, they almost always stop nagging.

Students with Two Homes

If your parents/guardians live in two different homes, the Sunday Night Conference is a critical strategy for you to use with both parents.

Take a few minutes to speak with each parent. If possible, have both parents on the phone line with you. Talk to them about your schedule for the week and make sure they both know about any practices you have after school, big tests, or projects that you have coming up. Double-check when you will visit the other parent and who will be picking you up from soccer practice, etc.

This conference is the single best thing you can do for yourself when you call two places 'home.'

I have had countless parents and students tell me that taking a few minutes to plan their week together at the beginning of the week has been the greatest strategy they have ever tried. It really does work!

During Class

Time Saving Tip

Minimize homework time by using every second in school:

- Pay attention in class so you don't have to relearn everything when you sit down to do your homework.

- During the moments you are stuck waiting in class, open your binder and reread your notes from all of your classes. A few minutes in class saves a lot of study time at home!

Keep a pen in the rings of your planner so you can record homework, due dates, test dates, and other critical information right away. You are more likely to use a planner regularly if you do not have to search through your bag every time you need to write something down.

Keep your planner accessible. The best place to keep your planner is on your desk, or at least on top of the rest of your belongings under the desk. Once again, you are more likely to use a planner if you do not have to dig for it.

Record your homework as it is assigned in class. Also make note of the books you will need to take home. Do not wait until the end of the day to write down assignments because you are likely to record the *wrong* assignment or not record anything at all.

End of School Day, Before Going Home

Sometime before you go home from school (perhaps in the final moments of your last class or on the bus), take a few seconds to plan when you will work on homework that evening. Review your planner notes and write down how much time you will need for each assignment so you can appropriately plan how much time you will need.

Check your planner before you go home to be sure you have all of the books you need. This will take no more than five seconds if you have the current page marked with a binder clip and your planner easily accessible in your arms or book bag.

At Home, After School

Stick to your schedule! Share it with your parents so that they know you are being responsible and will be less likely to "bug" you about your homework. If something comes up, or you simply get off track, get back on track by thinking about your priorities and take care of your "rock" priorities first.

Stay on schedule by "powering down" during homework time. Using electronics will only delay your progress. Turn off cell phones (no calls or text-messages...save them for later), turn off the TV, radio, or iPod, and turn down the volume on your computer so that you do not hear every email that may be "popping" into your computer. Turning everything off may not sound very fun, but it will help you get your homework done much quicker. Do yourself the favor of avoiding the distractions, getting homework done on time, and then enjoying TV, music, phone calls, or texting later. (It's all about priorities!)

Time Saving Tip

Use a timer to help you stay focused while working on homework. Set the timer for the amount of time you think a homework assignment should take, and then work to "beat the clock." Of course, the point is not to rush your work, but to stay focused and avoid distractions.

Before Bedtime

Avoid rushed mornings by taking a minute before you go to bed to check your planner one last time: Did you get all forms signed? Is all of your homework in your bag? Do you have your lunch money? Is there anything else you needed to take care of?

Get everything you need ready, in your bag, and placed by the door before you go to bed. This simple habit will reduce morning craziness and will dramatically increase your feeling of preparedness in school the next day.

Keeping a Good Balance

Use your planner for organizing more than just schoolwork; record scheduled appointments, notes about family events, and goals for other areas of your life in your planner, too.

For Example…

A sample planner page is on page 31. The items in bold show what this student planned at the beginning of the week. Notice that one of her weekly goals was to shoot hoops and run three days this week. So, she plugged those items into her planner on Monday, Tuesday, and Thursday. She also has a TV program on Monday night that she does not want to miss, so she wrote that down, too. She also recorded some time for her to review her notes everyday. She is even reviewing her notes on Friday afternoon, but she is giving herself a break from all other homework Friday night.

On Monday, she recorded her homework in each class, as it was assigned, and in 8th hour she spent two minutes figuring out when she would get her homework done that night. Her schedule may get thrown off a bit, but if it does, she still has a structure to follow to help her stay focused and achieve her other goal of having at least two homework-free hours every night. Chances are good that if she follows her plan, she will have a few more hours of homework-free time, too!

A good planner should include both a monthly and weekly layout to accommodate long-term and short-term planning.

Planner images courtesy of www.actionagendas.com.

SAMPLE

Sept	3 Monday	4 Tuesday	5 Wednesday	6 Thursday	7 Friday	8 Saturday / 9 Sunday / Weekly Goals
1st hour	Page 161 # 2-20 all					**8 Saturday** — Get homework done this morning (2 hours?)
2nd hour	None					
3rd hour	Get Permission Slip Signed					
4th hour	None					
5th hour						
6th hour	Study for Chapter 4 Test on Thurs.					
7th hour	Read section 5.2. Questions pg. 109			Science test today		**9 Sunday** — Grandma's b-day
Other	Math book / Science book / Language Arts book					lunch 1 p.m.
3 p.m.	Snack	Movie Club Mtg. Snack	Snack	Snack	Snack	**Weekly Goals**
4 p.m.	Shoot hoops & run	Shoot hoops & run	Review all notes for 15 minutes/ Do Math	Shoot hoops & run	Review all notes for 15 minutes	- Shoot hoops and run three days this week
5 p.m.	Review all notes for 15 minutes/ Do Math	Review all notes for 15 minutes/ Do Math	Study 15 min. for Science test	Review all notes for 15 minutes/ Do Math	No other homework tonight!	- Review notes everyday
6 p.m.	Study Science 15 min. L. Arts HW (1 hr)	Study 20 min. for Science test				
7 p.m.					Football game	
8 p.m.	Watch TV Show at 8:30					- Have at least two hours of homework-free time every evening!
9 -10 p.m.	10:30 Read in bed/Sleep	10:30 Read in bed/Sleep	10:30 Read in bed/Sleep	10:30 Read in bed/ Sleep		

www.StudySkills.com

Sept	Monday	Tuesday	Wednesday	Thursday	Friday	Saturday
1st hour						
2nd hour						
3rd hour						
4th hour						
5th hour						
6th hour						
7th hour						
Other						
3 p.m.						
4 p.m.						
5 p.m.						
6 p.m.						
7 p.m.						
8 p.m.						
9 -10 p.m.						

Sunday

Weekly Goals

Selecting a Planner

One significant reason why many students do not like using a planner is that most planners on the market are more confusing than they are helpful! There are several things to consider when looking for a planner:

An effective planner for middle school, high school, college, and even professional life will have:

❶ A page to view an entire month at once, PLUS

❷ One week of planning space per page, or per two-page spread. This means that you should be able to see seven days worth of planning space without having to turn one page.

❸ Space to record weekly goals is very helpful, but not necessary.

A planner should always be easy to carry. The easier it is to transport, the more likely you are to use it.

Not sure where to buy a good planner?
Go to www.StudySkills.com and click on "products" to find reliable planner resources.

Bulky planners are too impractical to carry around and keep accessible.

Inappropriate planners have:

❶ A bulky binder, leather, or fabric cover. These planners are too big to carry around easily. If it is inconvenient to carry a planner, you simply will not use it.

❷ Only one day of planning space per page; this layout makes weekly planning impossible.

Some Cautions About Using Mobile Phones

I used to completely discourage the use of mobile phones as "planners" for two reasons: first, it was difficult to enter information in them. Secondly, it was challenging to see several dates at one time, making weekly planning impossible. However, smart phones are changing the game and these issues are no longer "issues."

The single best advantage to using a smart phone is that it is always accessible and rarely out of your reach. Using a phone also allows you to program alarms and SMS messages as reminders, which can be very useful for managing schoolwork and after-school activities.

However, there are some things you should keep in mind if you plan to use your phone as your planner:

① **Only use your phone IF your school allows it to be used in class for recording assignments, dates, etc.** If your school does not allow the use of phones in class, you should stick with a traditional planner.

② **All of the guidelines from this chapter still apply:** you should still review your week on Sunday evening and coordinate with your family, record homework as it assigned in class, check your list of assignments before you leave school at the end of the day, etc.

③ **Alarms and SMS reminders should *only* be used as "back-up" reminders.** You should review your calendar and assignment list weekly and daily to be aware of your responsibilities. This process prevents them from becoming "last-minute" and taking twice as long to handle.

Planners: A Lifelong Tool

Developing the habit of using a planner does take some effort, but the payoff is well worth it! **Not only will you find that schoolwork is easier to manage, your grades will automatically improve, and your stress level will decrease because YOU will be in control.** Learning these management skills now will make life in the "real world" much more easier and will allow you to achieve great success!

*S*et goals
-Summary-

1 The most important part of doing well in school, and in life, is to set goals for what you want to accomplish.

2 Understanding your priorities helps you identify what is really important in your life, which is how you determine your goals.

3 Learning how to rank your priorities in life helps you make sure you have time for work and fun.

4 The key to accomplishing your goals is to *plan* for action.

*O*rganize

section

3

Organize

Check all statements below that apply to you:

_____ Have you ever brought the wrong notebook or folder to class or home for homework?

_____ Have you ever misplaced a homework assignment that you know you did?

_____ When you look inside your bag and locker, is there a sea of randomly stashed papers staring back at you?

_____ Do you have a hard time keeping your room neat and organized?

_____ Do you ever feel rushed and frustrated getting ready for school?

You will find solutions to these problems, and much more, in the following section.

For every minute spent organizing, an hour is earned.

What are some terms you might associate with someone who is *dis*organized? Scattered, confused, forgetful, puzzled, bewildered, absentminded, frustrated, messy, jumbled… Do any of these words paint a picture of an effective and successful student?

Absolutely not!

Being organized is the vital foundation for achieving success in school. Contrary to popular belief, organizing skills are not something you are either born with or without; they are skills that are learned and developed over time. Certainly, some people are more inclined to being organized than others, but *anyone* can learn strategies to create some order in their lives.

As always, the goal of this section is to share some easy strategies that will only take a short time to do, but will *save* a lot of time and hassle in the long run. In this section, you will learn about a great system for organizing all of your papers and notebooks for school. It is simple, cheap, and easy to use. You will also learn some tips for keeping your room, book bag, and locker in a neat, functional order. Finally, you will review many different ways to organize your time by developing simple routines. The more organized you are, the more you simplify your life. The more you simplify your life, the more efficient you become.

What are some terms you may associate with an *organized* person? Neat, orderly, got-it-together, calm, accomplished, capable, successful, prepared…These words can all describe YOU!

chapter 5

Organize Your Papers
Organize Your Space
Organize Your Time

One of the most common problems students complain about is managing all of their papers, folders, and notebooks. Many parents and teachers would agree; they get frustrated when their students cannot keep track of assignments, find completed work, or keep their folders and bags in order.

Do any of these scenarios sound familiar to you?

- ❑ "I know I did my homework, but I can't find it now!"

- ❑ "Oh, no...I brought my science notebook home instead of my math notebook!"

- ❑ "My bag is so heavy, sometimes I think my back will break!"

- ❑ "My spiral notebooks get caught on everything; the bottom of my bag, my clothes, each other...they are very annoying."

- ❑ "I get so many papers and don't have any time to put them away, so they all fall to the bottom of my bag and get crushed."

If you can relate to any of these comments, you are not alone!

Most students simply have too much "stuff" to deal with. Typically, students will have one folder and one notebook for each of their classes; That can be up to 8 folders and 8 notebooks...16 items combined! No wonder papers end up all over the place! Wouldn't it be nice if you could condense all of your papers, folders, and notebooks down to one easy-to-manage binder? ...You can!

The S·O·A·R™ Binder System

The SOAR™ Binder System solves all of the problems described on the previous page; it is a very simple and easy way to keep school-work organized! It consists of one 1-inch binder that houses folders and notebooks for *all* of your classes.

You are probably wondering:

> **"How can I keep seven inches of notebooks and folders in a one-inch binder? It'll never work!"**

It may seem unlikely, but it is possible. This system has made a significant difference for hundreds of students, from grade school to grad school.

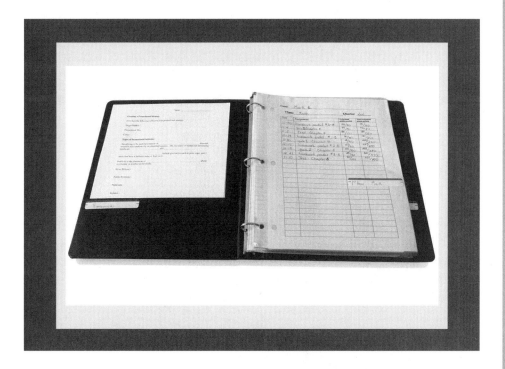

I can't believe how much easier it is for me to keep my papers organized. Since I started using the Binder, I have not lost one assignment! My parents are so excited and I feel so much better about school. -Thank you!

- Michael Zabik, 9th grade student

"How does it work?"

A SOAR™ Binder replaces traditional folders and notebooks with plastic one-pocket folders and loose-leaf notebook paper. Each plastic folder holds papers for individual classes and acts as a divider for notes, which are placed behind the folder. At the end of each marking period, the folders are emptied into a simple 'home filing system' to keep the binder from getting overloaded. The binder travels with you to each class and goes home with you at the end of each day. You never have to worry about taking the wrong folder/notebook to class or home for homework because you only have to keep track of one item.

The SOAR™ Binder System is a perfect organizing solution when you live in two homes. You never have to worry about leaving a folder or notebook at the "other" house because everything is in in **one binder**, making it easier to keep papers and notes with you, regardless of where you are.

"How do I create a S∙O∙A∙R™ Binder?"

It is easy to put a SOAR™ Binder together. Simply get a few supplies, as listed on the next page, and follow the steps for assembling and using the binder. (You can also purchase SOAR™ Binder supplies by going to www.StudySkills.com and clicking on "products".) You can begin using this tomorrow and will instantly notice how much easier it will be to *get* and *stay* organized.

step 1

Gather Materials

- One, 1" diameter binder with pockets on the inside covers *

- One plastic folder for each individual class (Avery Binder Pockets work well)

- One file folder for each individual class

- Labels for each folder and binder pocket

- Loose-leaf notebook paper

* Anything larger than a 1" binder is too bulky to carry, and therefore less likely to be used. However, if you are *not* allowed to carry a bag in school, you may want to use a 1½" binder so you have room inside for a zipper case to hold pens, pencils, and other supplies.

step 2

Put the Pieces Together

- **Place the plastic folders in the binder rings.** The plastic folders work better than traditional folders because they are more durable. They also minimize bulk because you typically will only need one pocket for each class.

- **Place 20-30 sheets of notebook paper behind the last folder at the back of the binder.** As you need to take notes, you will use these notebook papers to write your notes and will then store your notes behind the folder for that class.

step 3

Label Folders in the Binder

- **Label your folders.** It is very important to label one folder for each class so you do not accidently put papers in the wrong place. A simple label can save a lot of frustration when you are rushed and need to find something in your binder quickly.

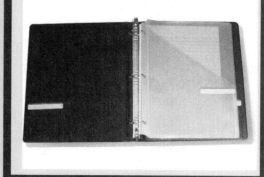

- **Label the front pocket of the binder "Homework" and the back pocket of the binder "Miscellaneous."**

Create a 'Home Filing System'

step 4

- **Label one file folder for each of your classes and store the file folders in a safe place at home.** A 'safe place' may be a small file crate, a shoe box under your bed, a specific drawer in your desk, or even in your parents' filing cabinet. The important thing is to determine one specific place so you will not lose them!

- **Store binder over-flow in these file folders.** Periodically (about 1 or 2 times per quarter), remove papers from your binder and put them in the file folders. Do not throw away any papers until after you have received your final grade for each class; these papers will help you create a good study guide for big unit tests or final exams and will also help you prove your grade if a mistake shows up on your report card.

"How do I use the S·O·A·R™ Binder System?"

The magic of the SOAR™ Binder System is in how you use it! Follow the tips below:

Using the Binder in School

NEVER put loose papers inside your bookbag! Instead of cramming papers into your bag, just slide them into the front of your binder. Later, when you have a few seconds, you can put the papers in their correct folders.

Don't trash your book bag! When you are in
a hurry, simply slide papers under the front cover of
your binder instead of stashing them loosely in your bag.

Keep your binder easily accessible througout the day. Like your planner, keep it on your desk or on top of all of your belongings under the desk. Once again, you are much more likely to use it if you do not have to dig through several things to access it.

Put ALL papers that need your attention at home in the front pocket of the binder. This includes homework papers, notes for your parents, forms that need to be signed, items you want to leave at home, etc. This will save you time at home because you will not have to rifle through several folders to find your homework pages.

Use the back pocket of the binder for "miscellaneous" items. Sometimes you have to hang on to papers that are not for a specific class, so they may not have a specific folder. Items such as school fundraiser information or a health form for P.E. can be placed in the back pocket of your binder for safe keeping.

 ## Using the Binder at Home

Take 60 seconds to put stray papers into their correct folders. If you were rushed in school and had to stash a few papers in the front of your binder, take a few seconds to put them away when you sit down to do your homework. A few seconds each night will save you a lot of time and frustration later.

As you finish homework pages, immediately put them away in the correct folders. Do not wait until you finish *all* of your homework before you put your papers away; this increases the chances of papers getting mixed up with other items in your home, put in the wrong folder, or simply forgotten.

Clean out your binder 1 or 2 times per quarter and put the 'old' papers in your file folders. It cannot be emphasized enough...do not throw any papers away until you get your report card! Your old papers are a gem for making study guides and will help you correct any possible errors your teacher may have made in recording your grades.

Common Questions About Using the S·O·A·R™ Binder System

Q: "My teacher requires a separate folder/binder for her class. I don't think she'll let me use the S·O·A·R™ Binder System."

A: Most teachers request specific materials to help ensure that students have a method for organizing supplies for their class. Once you show her how your binder works, she is likely to allow an exception. In eight years of teaching this method, I know of only one teacher who insisted on a separate binder for her class. If this *should* happen to you, abide by your teacher's wishes, but continue to use the S·O·A·R™ Binder System for all of your other classes.

Q: "What if I can't get all of my papers to fit into a 1-inch binder?"

A: You should have no problems fitting everything you need into one binder. Remember to clean out your folders and notes at least once per quarter (possibly twice). Also, make sure you are only using loose-leaf notebook paper and NOT storing spiral notebooks in your binder.

Q: "My teacher often collects our notebooks. He will want me to have a spiral notebook...what do I do?"

A: Ask your teacher if you can simply staple your notebook pages together and turn in the packet of papers when he collects notebooks. As mentioned earlier, teachers are usually quite receptive to helping students get and stay organized, so you are not likely to have a problem.

chapter 6

Organize Your Papers
Organize Your Space
Organize Your Time

Cluttered Spaces = Cluttered Minds

Now that your folders and notebooks are in order, it's time to put your space in order, too. The condition of your bedroom, book bag, and locker plays a big role in your efficiency in school. Messy spaces can be overwhelming and distracting, not to mention the perfect place to lose homework and other important things.

A Place for Everything and Everything in It's Place

With two younger brothers and a busy household, keeping things organized was a fairly low priority for my family as I was growing up. It seems like we were always scouring the house trying to find our shoes, keys, and other personal items. And, it was usually impossible to find things like scissors, measuring tape, and markers.

However, there was always one thing that, in over 20 years, was never lost; the flashlight. Why, you might ask, could we always find the flashlight? Because we had a very specific place designated for it. The flashlight was fairly heavy-duty with a long handle, so Dad cut a piece of PVC pipe down to about 10 inches, screwed it to the bottom of the shelf in our hall closet, and stored the flashlight in the pipe. It was the one piece of equipment we could *always* find.

As this example illustrates, the key to *keeping* your space organized is having a specific, designated space for all of your belongings.

The information in this chapter will help you create a home for all of your things and help you keep your space well organized. The chapter is not about being perfectly clean, but about having a general sense of control when it comes to managing your belongings.

Organize *Mission Control*: Your Room

Your room is your personal Mission Control; the central space from which you organize your life. Having a cluttered and chaotic room can have a dramatic effect on how you perform in school. When your room is organized, you are more likely to keep track of your assignments and be more efficient with homework, getting ready for school, and doing just about anything else. Most significantly, you will have a greater feeling of control in your life.

Depending on how messy your room is, it may take a little while to get it cleaned and organized in the first place. However, the following steps will guide you through a process that will make it easy to keep your room organized for the long-haul.

step 1   Remove the Stuff You Don't Need

Decluttering is a little easier said than done, yet is vital to getting organized. In our disposable society, we accumulate items so fast that our possessions can easily overtake our lives if we are not careful. How can you easily get rid of the extra things you don't need?

Label four large boxes (or garbage bags): "Trash", "Donations", "Storage", and "Somewhere Else."
Just as the labels suggest:

 The **Trash Box** is for garbage.

 The **Donations Box** is for used clothes, toys, CDs, etc. that are in good condition and can be donated to charity. (This is a great way to help others and to re-cycle at the same time.)

 The **Storage Box** is for items you want to keep, but do not need to store in your room. (Ask for your parents' permission before you store your belongings anywhere else in the house.)

 The **Somewhere Else Box** is for items that belong somewhere else in the house. Instead of wasting a lot of time by running found items around the rest of the house, collect them all together and deliver them to their correct place all at once.

Storage Tip

If you must put items in 'storage,' clearly label the outside of all containers that you are storing. One way to keep storage stuff under control is to limit yourself to one large box, especially for memorabilia. If an item does not fit in your box, then it is time to get rid of something.

step 2

Group Similar Items Together

Gather similar items together to help identify a logical home for them. As you may recall, establishing a place for everything is the key to keeping your space organized.

Do you have a spot to store the following:

- ❑ CDs, DVDs, and related equipment?
- ❑ Stuffed animals?
- ❑ Trophies and awards?
- ❑ Notes and pictures of friends?
- ❑ Sports equipment?
- ❑ Music equipment (instruments, etc.)?
- ❑ School supplies and your 'Home Filing System'?
- ❑ Books?
- ❑ Computer, computer supplies, and other electronic devices?
- ❑ Clothes? (Are they over-stuffed in drawers or closets?)
- ❑ Supplies/materials for a special hobby that you have?

Look around your room…are there additional items that did not fit in any of the previous categories? It is okay to have a group of items that do not seem to go with anything else...these will be the last items you put away.

step 3

Find a Place for Everything

Creating a specific place for everything is the key step to *keeping* your room organized. Consider the following storage suggestions:

Space under the bed is good for storing items such as shoes, CDs, and bedding. Simply put items in containers that will slide out so you can easily access everything. There are several storage containers on the market for use under standard beds.

Use the tops of tall bookcases and dressers. These are good places to store things that you do not need to access regularly, such as stuffed animals and trophies.

Look up! Many closets have a lot of unused space above the top shelf. Consider storing large items there such as luggage and sleeping bags. (Would the sleeping bag fit inside the luggage?)

A large bulletin board is a great place to post pictures, notes from friends, special mementos, ribbons, and other 2-dimensional items. In addition to keeping desk and dresser tops free of clutter, they can add a nice dimension to your room. You can dress up a standard bulletin board with fabric (like the one pictured to the left) or by spray painting it to match your room.

Trunks provide great storage and added seating space for visiting friends. However, trunk space should not be used to store small items that will easily get lost in the deep space. Consider using trunks for storing shoes, extra bedding, board games, bulky sweaters, sport/music equipment, or other large items.

Plastic crates are good for items such as books, CDs, school supplies, electronics accessories, and small sports equipment. Crates are ideal storage pieces because their utility is flexible; their use can change as your needs and interests change. Secondly, the stackable nature of the crates makes good use of vertical storage, which is commonly unused space.

Organize Your Study Space

Whether you typically do your homework in your bedroom, in the kitchen, near the computer, or anywhere else, it is important that you have a place with few distractions so you can get homework done quickly.

Some tips for maximizing your study space:

Keep a bucket or basket supplied with pens, pencils, a stapler, tape, paper, dictionary, grammar guide, and thesaurus. This container can easily move with you if you need to do some of your homework in another room (e.g. near the computer).

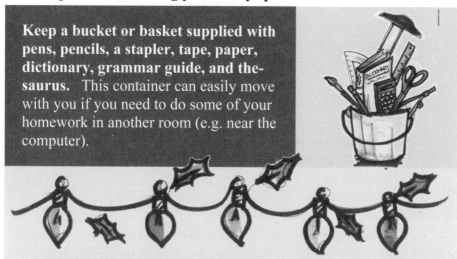

Make your space comfortable. Snaz it up with a poster, flowers, holiday lights… Making your study space more inviting will help to make the process of doing homework a bit more enjoyable.

Keep lighting and temperature at comfortable levels. The lighting should be comfortable for you...not too dim, but not too bright. Likewise, the room temperature should not be extreme. Lighting and temperature play a big role in helping you stay focused.

Play baroque music to help you concentrate. Baroque is a style of classical music that is written in the same mathematical pattern as your resting heart-rate. It is not a "magic" solution for concentration, but it helps your mind and body work more in-sync, which is calming and minimizes distractions. If you live in an active house, it will help you drown out background noise. It also works well *as* background noise if you cannot concentrate when it is 'too quiet.' To find a CD, ask for baroque music in your local music store, or search for baroque on-line.

Organize Your Locker

First and foremost, keep trash out of your locker! When you are in a rush for class, you can't afford to be rifling through a bunch of junk trying to find your books.

Get in and out of your locker quickly by storing morning books flat and afternoon books standing upright. This tactic helps you identify and grab books quickly, not only because they are neatly organized, but because it is easier to pull textbooks out of two smaller, lighter piles than one tall, heavy pile. If you have covers on your text books, label the spines clearly so you don't grab the wrong book.

Keep morning books flat and after-noon books standing upright.

As you stop at your locker throughout the day, place books you need for homework on the floor of your locker, under your coat (just be sure you don't have water or melting snow on your coat that will drip onto your books).

Organize Your Book Bag

The greatest weapon against a book bag in disarray is the SOAR™ Binder! The primary cause of a disorganized bag is the collection of loose papers that collect in the bottom, getting crushed and crumpled by the rest of your belongings. Always use your binder to keep papers in order. It cannot be emphasized enough, even if you are in a rush and don't have time to put papers in their proper folders, at least slide them inside the front of your binder to put away later. This simple step will save you many hours of searching for papers in the depths of your book bag and prevent you from loosing points on lost homework that you know you did!

Before you head home at the end of the school day, take one last look in your locker to make sure you haven't left behind books or supplies that you need for homework. Likewise, before you go to bed at night, always check your bag to make sure you have everything you need for school the next day, *especially* your binder.

Conclusion

All of the information in this chapter is designed to give you some pointers for keeping your belongings under control. You do not have to be a 'neat freak' to stay organized, but should simply identify places for your possessions and try to keep them in place. Like everything else, it will be easier for some than others, but is a great habit to develop. Learning how to organize your things will benefit you for the rest of your life, saving time and allowing you to be more productive. It is a wonderful feeling when you have control over your clutter, instead of your clutter having control over you.

> *It is a wonderful feeling when you have control over your clutter, instead of your clutter having control over you.*

Now that your space is organized, you are in a position to begin working more efficiently. The next chapter will provide you with even more resources for efficiency (i.e. more personal time) as you learn strategies for organizing your time.

chapter 7

Organize Your Papers
Organize Your Space
Organize Your Time

You only have 24 hours in one day and likely have a lot of things you want to do during that time. To help ensure that you have time for your fun 'pebble' priorities, it is important to organize your time. Of course, you have to be flexible in order to accommodate unexpected events. However, there are several things you can do to use your time more efficiently.

The process of 'organizing your time' emerges automatically as you follow portions of the program already described in this book. In many ways, this chapter is a review of previously covered strategies, but a few of them will be revisited in the interest of keeping your time under control.

Develop Routines

One important principle about organizing your time is to develop routines for things that you do regularly. The more automatic certain tasks are for you, the easier they will be and the less time they will take.

7-21

...is the number of attempts required to develop a habit.

Research suggests that a person has to do something 7 to 21 times before it becomes a habit, so developing routines can take time, but the time you save in the long-run is worth it. There are a few specific routines that can especially maximize your time:

Use a planner everyday! Record all of the things you need to do at home *or* in school. Don't forget to write down test dates, project due dates, books you need to take home, and permission slips that need to be signed. Make it a point to look at it when you get home and double-check it before you go to bed.

Initiate "Sunday Night Meetings" with your parents. As mentioned on page 27, tell your parents about your sports practices/games, due dates, supplies you may need for a special project, etc. Be sure to ask them what their schedule looks like for the week. (They'll be impressed with your consideration of their schedule.) If your parents are separated, be sure you talk to *both* of them about the upcoming week.

Avoid rushed and chaotic mornings. Mornings are hectic for most people. "I was so busy this morning, I forgot my homework on the kitchen table" is one of the top excuses for not turning homework in on time. The solution is simple...prepare the night before.

Before you go to bed on a school night, you should:

❏ Put all of your papers in your binder and make sure they are in the correct folder.

❏ Double-check your planner to make sure you took care of everything that needed your attention; homework, notes that need to be signed, field trip money, etc.

❏ Gather your binder, planner, all of your books, lunch money, other necessary supplies and place them in your bag. Don't forget about any gear you may need for things such as dance class or track practice.

❏ Put your bag by the door you will exit in the morning.

❏ Pick out your clothes for the next day to save the time of deliberating over what to wear and to prevent a last-minute search for your favorite pair of jeans or shoes.

Make your week even more efficient... gathering your clothes once per week is a lot more efficient than doing it everyday.

Maximize Your Time

Have you ever noticed how much of your time is "wasted" in a day? There are several ways you can maximize this otherwise unused time:

Take advantage of "down-time" in school. Some studies speculate that only 50-60% of a student's school day is actually spent on productive lessons or related activities. The rest of the time is spent taking attendance, waiting for other students, school announcements, classroom interruptions, etc. Take advantage of this time! Open your binder and review your notes from a few previous classes, pull out your math assignment and get a few problems done, read the next section of your science text book, etc. Many students manage to complete most, if not all, of their homework in school by using this down-time to their advantage.

Take advantage of "down-time" during after school activities. Just as you can find windows of time during school, you can often find small chunks of time while waiting for activities after school.

Do you have a long bus ride? Even if you spend 15 minutes working on some homework or reviewing your notes, it's 15 more minutes you'll have for yourself at home. Of course, sometimes it is nice to socialize with friends on the bus ride to and from school, which is okay; it will help you relax a bit after school and get refreshed to start your homework earlier.

Do your homework as early in the afternoon as possible. While it is important to give yourself a little break after school, the break should be no more than 45 minutes. As soon as you can start your homework, the more quickly it will get done. If you wait until later in the evening, you will slow down and not be as efficient.

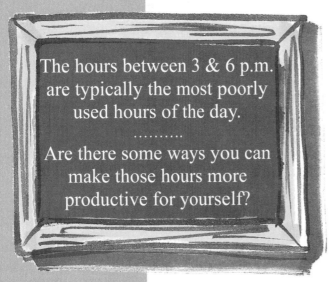

The hours between 3 & 6 p.m. are typically the most poorly used hours of the day.
....
Are there some ways you can make those hours more productive for yourself?

Power down! Turn off your cell phone, TV, radio, and computer. No matter who you are, there is always the temptation to do two things at once, but it is impossible for you to concentrate on more than one thing at a time (your brain is not capable of processing more than one set of audio or visual input at one time). Therefore, do yourself the favor of getting your homework done and out of the way, then you can enjoy your electronics without the stress of homework to bog you down!

Conclusion

No one is ever perfect at managing their time, but this chapter covers some of the things you can do to make better use of your time more often.

Now that you have established your goals and organized all aspects of your life, it is time to learn some easy and effective study strategies in the next section, *Ask questions*.

*O*rganize
-Summary-

1 **Organizing skills are learned. They are *not* skills that some people are born with and others without.** Learning how to organize will help you gain a lot of confidence and a greater sense of control in your life, making success easier to achieve.

2 **The SOAR™ Binder System is a simple solution for keeping notes, assignments, and all school-related materials in one convenient location.** Among many benefits: it prevents homework from getting lost, keeps your book bag clean, and reduces the weight you have to carry around by eliminating spiral notebooks.

3 **Clutter creates a distracting environment.** Keeping your space organized will help you be much more efficient and successful in school. The key to keeping clutter under control is to create a specific place for each of your belongings.

4 **Create more time for "fun stuff" in your life.** Developing routines and making use of otherwise wasted time will allow you to have more time for your "water" and "pebble" priorities.

Ask questions

a strategy for...

section 4

Ask questions

Check all statements below that apply to you:

_____ I sometimes do not know what questions to ask in class.

_____ I have a hard time remembering information when I read a text book.

_____ When I have to write a paper, I don't even know where to start.

_____ I think I could do a better job of taking notes and using my notes to study for tests.

_____ I don't take tests very well. I think I know the information, but I'm often disappointed with my scores.

You will find solutions to these problems, and much more, in the following section.

100% of all shots _not_ taken...

are missed.

You may be asking yourself, "What do questions have to do with study skills?" The answer is: A LOT! When you learn how to use questions effectively, you can improve your grades while reducing study time because you will study more efficiently.

"How does that work?"

You must first understand how your brain works…

Your brain is like a file cabinet. When information first enters your brain, it goes into your short-term memory. Short-term memory is like a jumbled, unorganized drawer of a file cabinet that has a small capacity and over-flows quickly. This is how your short-term memory works; it fills up quickly and dumps information often (in approximately 24-hour cycles).

In order to remember what you learn, you need to transfer information from the jumbled mess of your short-term memory and place it in your long-term memory. You do this by reviewing content at least once within 24 hours of learning information, and then reviewing it again periodically.

Of course, there is more to long-term memory than simply reviewing information. You also need to be able to recall what you have learned. You might imagine that all information you put in your long-term memory needs to be in carefully filed folders so you can find the information when you need it, like when you are taking a test.

This is where "asking questions" comes into play. When you ask questions to help you process new information, you connect the new information to things you already know. This process of developing connections is how you neatly arrange information in your long-term memory and make it available for recall.

The following chapters will show you how you can apply the skill of asking questions to help you interact with teachers, read text books, write papers, take notes, and study for tests.

Your brain is like a file cabinet; it stores information you learn and keeps it organized so you can recall it when you need it.

Asking questions is a powerful strategy for helping you organize the things you learn.

chapter 8

Interacting with Teachers

"Why do I need to worry about interacting with my teachers?"

Complete the activity below to discover the answer to that question.

Directions: Draw the floor plan (bird's eye view) of one of your classrooms in the box below. Use the key to represent the appropriate people and furniture in the room. (See page 66 for an example.)

Key

☒ = student desk

☑ = teacher desk

↑ = door (entrance to room)

❏ = classroom closet and/or cabinets

◼ = table

▱ = file cabinet

☺ = you

✪ = your teacher

Look at the map you just created. If you drew everything within a reasonable scale, you should notice that you represent one *small* part of a much larger classroom.

Think about this….

Your teachers have to be accountable for teaching and supervising a lot of people at one time, usually 20-36 students per class. For most middle and high-school teachers, that adds up to 100-150 students per day and that number only increases for most college instructors! This is a tremendous responsibility for one person to maintain. In order to most effectively help you, your teachers first need your help.

> *You are one small part of a much larger classroom…*
>
> *It is up to you to help your teachers know who you are.*

Asking Questions

One single teacher cannot possibly offer adequate attention to over 100 students everyday. Therefore, *you* need to do something to distinguish yourself from the crowd in a positive way. All it takes is raising your hand to ask a reasonable question once in a while (more than just, "Can I go to the bathroom?"), or contributing respectfully to class discussions. If you're not comfortable asking questions in class, stay after class occasionally to ask your teacher for clarification on an assignment or to check your grades. Some of the following chapters, such as *Reading Text Books* and *Taking Notes* will offer additional tips to help you formulate good questions in class; simply look for the "Teacher Talking Point" icon.

"Why bother?"

Simply asking a few questions or contributing occasionally to class discussions will let your teachers know that you are a conscientious student and that you care about your work. These simple gestures draw teachers' attention to you, helping you stand out in the sea of faces that they interact with everyday. 99.9% of teachers are in their profession to help students and they relish the opportunity to assist those who are really interested in succeeding. Respectful, high-aspiring students are rare, so stand out!

"How can talking to my teachers help my grades?"

There are many benefits in helping your teachers get to know you. For one, teachers who know that you are diligent about your work will be more likely to grade your assignments with some leniency. For example, they may be more likely to give you half credit on an incorrect math problem or be willing to overlook a few spelling errors on a writing assignment because they know that you put forth a lot of effort. At the end of a marking period, teachers may also add a couple points to the total scores of students whom, they believe, deserve a little boost. Obviously, students who are disrespectful or act like they do not care about their work are not likely to *earn* this little bonus.

Developing a positive relationship with your teachers is also beneficial when you need a letter of recommendation or are looking for a job. A powerful letter of recommendation from a teacher can put you over the top of another candidate when applying for college, scholarships, and completing job applications. Likewise, teachers are often great leads for part-time jobs and other opportunities; they are frequently asked by business-owners to recommend "responsible and reliable" students for hire. Employers like to have recommendations from teachers who can hand-pick their best students, those who have demonstrated responsibility and a respectful attitude in class.

> **Teacher Talking Points**
>
> Have you ever been afraid to ask a question in class because you tuned out for a while and think the teacher may have just answered your question?
>
> This happens to everyone, even adults. When you are in this situation, simply raise your hand and say, "You may have already answered this, but I missed it. Can you please explain…?" Most teachers will appreciate your respectfulness and will be happy to answer your question.

"I have a hard time paying attention in class. Is there anything I can do to help me focus (or stay awake)?"

Yes, there are several things you can do to help keep yourself focused: First, nothing beats a good night's rest and a nutritious breakfast. These two things alone can greatly improve concentration in class. However, we all know that there are days when that is not possible, or in some cases, is not enough. The next best alternative is to improve your circulation. Your body's circulation begins to slow down after you have been sitting for about 45 minutes. This is usually the time when people begin to feel restless or drowsy. Some ways to rev up your circulation and boost concentration are:

Take a brief walk. If it is possible to get up and walk around for a few minutes, you can get your blood pumping and wake up your system immediately.

Adjust your posture. If you are not able to get out of your seat, try improving your posture. After sitting for a while, your shoulders have probably slumped over a bit, your legs may be crossed, you may have slouched down in your chair, etc. All of these positions reduce the efficiency of your circulatory system. So, sit up straight, uncross your legs, lean slightly forward, and smile. (You'll feel better.)

Take some deep breaths. This works best after you've adjusted your posture, as described above. Once you've straightened yourself up, inhale as deeply and slowly as you can, hold your breath for as long as you can, and then exhale even more slowly. Do this a few times to revive the oxygen in your system.

Stretch your arms and legs. Again, adjust your posture, then S-T-R-E-E-E-E-T-C-H your arms and legs as much as you can without disrupting class.

Stretch your eye muscles. Sometimes tired eyes can make the rest of your body feel fatigued, too. To stretch your eyes muscles: First, close your eyes and gently massage them over your eyelids for ten-20 seconds. Keep your eyes closed and roll your eyeballs up towards the inside of your head, holding them in place for ten seconds. While you continue to close your eyes, roll your eyeballs down as if you were trying to see your teeth. Hold for another ten seconds. Finally, keep your lids closed and roll your eyes up so they are facing directly in front of you, then open your eyes. Repeat as needed.

The "T" Zone

The "T" Zone designates the approximate area in a classroom where you are most likely to catch your teacher's attention. As the diagram below illustrates, the "T" Zone is the front row and the one or two columns directly in front of where your teacher usually stands. Any of the desks highlighted by the "T" are within the zone.

"Why is this the best place to sit?"

When teachers are facilitating class discussions, they often have many things to think about and coordinate in their mind. Therefore, they tend to respond to the first students they notice. The "T" Zone represents the area that naturally captures a person's attention first.

It sounds a little quirky, but it is true. In your classes, pay attention to who is called upon by teachers. You will probably notice that more students in the "T" Zone are called upon than students sitting elsewhere in the room.

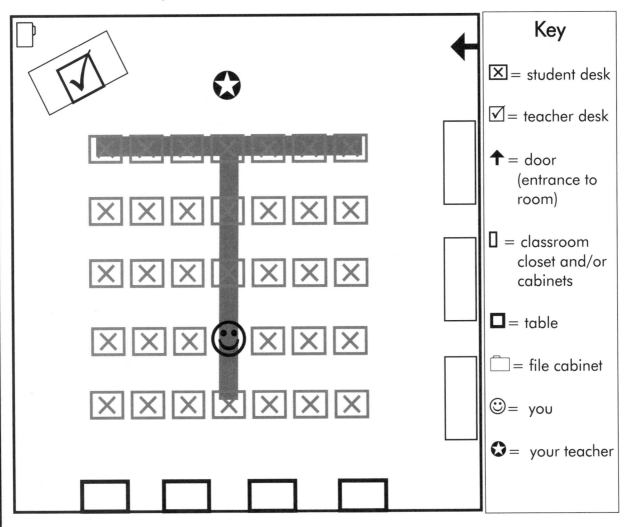

Key

☒ = student desk

☑ = teacher desk

↑ = door (entrance to room)

▯ = classroom closet and/or cabinets

▮ = table

▱ = file cabinet

☺ = you

✪ = your teacher

chapter 9

Reading Text Books

Have you ever spent a long time reading something, only to have no recollection of what you just read? This "brain black-out" is common, especially when reading a text book that is of little interest to you.

There are some quick things you can do to improve your comprehension when reading text books. To illustrate why it works, complete the following activity:

Directions:

❶ Turn to page 118 and look at the picture on that page for ONLY 5 seconds. Then move on to step 2.

❷ Now, turn to page 123 and answer as many questions as you can.

❸ Turn back to the picture on page 118 to check your answers.

❹ Record the number of correct answers you had after your *first* attempt: _____

"What's the Point?"

Most people approach text book reading in the same way you were instructed to look at the picture on page 118; with no idea what to look for! Wouldn't it have been easier if you had read the questions you were expected to answer *first*?

Of course!

Then you would have had a *purpose* when looking at the picture and would have been able to answer the questions more quickly, with much less confusion. **This improved speed and enhanced comprehension can also be accomplished when you read!**

Priming Your Brain: Developing a Purpose for Reading

Before a painter can paint something, she needs to prime it so the paint will stick to the surface. Primer is a sticky, paint-like substance that helps keep paint from flaking off surfaces.

You must also prime your brain before you read to help new information stick to it! It only takes a few minutes before you begin reading, but those few minutes will dramatically increase your comprehension.

Grab one of your text books, find a section to read, and try each of the following steps as you read them.

 step 1

***Read* all pictures and graphs in the entire reading selection.** Look at each picture, read the caption, and ask yourself, "Why is this here?" Look at graphs, tables, and charts and challenge yourself to figure out what the information in those graphics is about (spend approximately 20 seconds per picture or graph).

Purpose

Most pictures and graphs in textbooks are printed in color, which is costly to publish. Therefore, publishing companies carefully select visuals that best summarize the important parts of a topic. In fact, the black-and-white text usually does not describe new points, but simply adds details to the pictures and other visuals.

 step 2

Read the questions at the end of the chapter or reading selection.

Purpose

After "reading" the pictures, you may find that you already know the answers to some of these summary questions. Even if you don't know the answers, the process of reading the questions help prime your brain with a purpose for reading. This will focus your brain while reading and ultimately increase your speed and comprehension.

 step 3

Begin reading the text. As you read, turn the headings into questions.

Purpose

This process of turning headings into questions, once again, helps keep your brain focused, increasing reading speed and comprehension. It also helps your brain develop connections, which is important for recall.

Pictures are another powerful tool for developing recall because our brains are programmed to remember visual images better than anything else. While you read, the more associations you can make with visuals such as photographs and charts, the more you will understand and remember the content of the text.

Time Saving Tip

Read your text book before your teacher covers each section in class.

This strategy will give you some background knowledge to help you:

- Stay awake during class because you will actually have a clue about what is going on.
- Ask educated questions that will enhance your learning and impress your teacher.
- Save study time by making the most of your class time. If you come to class with some exposure to the topic of discussion, you'll understand lectures with greater ease and you will learn the information much more quickly, dramatically reducing study time at home.

 step 4

Answer the questions at the end of the chapter or reading selection.

Purpose

Review the summary questions to reinforce what you just learned.

Note: If you are *required* to answer the summary questions, try to include drawings, symbols, or other visuals with your answers to increase your retention.

If the questions are not assigned, you do not need to write out the answers. (Writing may increase your retention a bit, but it may turn you off to the method.) However, you will benefit from at least imagining a visual representation for each answer.

These four steps are all you need to do to read faster and with greater understanding. After practicing this method for the first time, it should only take about five additional minutes to do these strategies when reading.

After you follow this process once, you will immediately notice an increase in your comprehension. If you continue to use these strategies every time you read a text book, your total reading speed (and comprehension) will increase dramatically over the course of just a few weeks.

"Why does it work?"

Every step in this process encourages your brain to make connections with the material that you are reading. The process of making connections is how we are able to 'file' new information into our long-term memory and then recall the information at a later time. In the end, you can save study time by becoming a quicker reader and also by learning the information after you read it the first time, rather than having to study, relearn, and memorize it later.

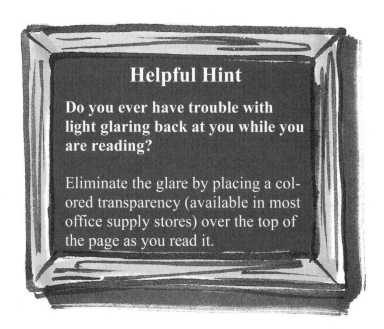

Helpful Hint

Do you ever have trouble with light glaring back at you while you are reading?

Eliminate the glare by placing a colored transparency (available in most office supply stores) over the top of the page as you read it.

chapter 10

Writing Papers

Now that you have practiced creating questions from your reading, you can use questions to help you write papers. Questions can help you explore your topic and arrange information into concise, organized paragraphs. The activities on the next two pages will illustrate how this works.

When you have to write a paper, brainstorm a list of questions that your paper should answer about the topic, then group similar questions together to create a few categories. The categories will become a guide while you write your paper. See the example below:

Assignment: Book Report

 step 1 — Brainstorm a list of questions that the report should answer.

1. Who are main characters?
2. What happens in the story?
3. Where does this story take place?
4. What is the title?
5. Who is the author?
6. When does this story take place?
7. What is the moral or theme?
8. Who is the hero? Villain?
9. How did the setting affect the story?
10. How does this story relate to things I've experienced?
11. How does this story relate to other books I've read?
12. What is the plot of the story?
13. Who solves the problem?

 step 2 — Create categories by grouping similar questions together.

1. What are some general pieces of information to introduce the book? (4,5,12)
2. Who are the main characters? Describe them. (1, 8)
3. Where does your story take place? What makes the setting unique and special for the story? (3,6,9)
4. What problems did the characters encounter? How did they resolve the problem? (2,13)
5. What is my conclusion? (7,10,11)

Note: The numbers in ( ) at the end of each question indicate items from the first column that were grouped together into broader questions.

step 3 — Start writing.

Start writing your paper by simply answering each of the questions listed above. As you write, the answers for each question will create a concise paragraph. This procedure helps you create an organized paper with well-defined paragraphs.

Usually, teachers will give you the categories that you need to address in your paper, so all you have to do is turn the categories into questions. See the next page for an example.

The research report on the next page is an actual assignment given to ninth grade students at a local high school and is probably similar to a writing assignment you have had to do before. The assignment lists several sub-topics that each student's report should cover. These sub-topics can easily be turned into questions. As you answer each question, you will be developing paragraphs for your report.

The example below has taken the sub-topics required for this paper and listed them in the first column. The second column illustrates how to turn these categories into questions. The primary reason for creating these questions is to 'prime your brain' so it will be more accurate in helping you identify relevant information for your paper.

<u>Directions:</u> Practice developing questions from the topics listed on the next page. The first three have been done as examples:

Assigned Sub-Topic...	Becomes a Question:
Introductory Paragraph	Are there any interesting points, stories, quotes, statistics, etc. that I may want to use as I introduce the topic of my paper?
Education/Skills	What skills and education are required for this career?
Description of the Work	What types of duties are required of this career?
Location & Setting	
Salary (Compensation)	
Closing Paragraph	

These questions are not only good sentence starters, they can help you organize notes for research papers. The 3-D Graphic Organizer on page 74 is an amazing tool that will help you easily organize research notes and write a quality paper.

Career Research Report

Choosing a career is an important decision because it will determine how you spend a significant portion of your life. This assignment, to research and write a report on a career that is of interest to you, is designed to help you discover some more information about a potential career for your future.

I. Report Guidelines

Your paper must be approximately 2-4 pages in length and include a Works Cited page.

II. Report Contents

Your report must address the following topics:

A. Opening Paragraph

Capture my attention with one or two interesting points, stories, quotes, statistics, etc. This paragraph should briefly describe the topic of your paper.

B. Education/Skills

Describe what type of education and/or training is required for this career including specific types of degrees or certifications. Explain special skills and personality traits that are well-suited for this career.

C. Description of the Work

Give a general description of the duties required of your career and describe a typical day at your job.

D. Location & Setting

Some careers are highly concentrated in certain parts of the country. Describe general locations where jobs in your field are located, the type of community you might live in, and the type of environment you might work in (medical, office, travel, working from home, etc.).

E. Salary/Compensation

Indicate what you expect to make in this career, including beginning wages, average income, and salary cap (the most you can make).

F. Closing Paragraph

Conclude your report with a summary about this career and a brief statement describing your opinion of this career, now that you have researched more details about it.

3-D Research Report Organizer

This report organizer is one of the most effective tools to help you organize your writing into logical, cohesive paragraphs. This technique has been used with students of all ages, from 3rd graders to college students, and it transforms writing skills instantly. In fact, I used a variation of this technique to write my 50-page Master's Thesis (see page 82 for more details). This is truly one strategy I wish I had known much earlier in life!

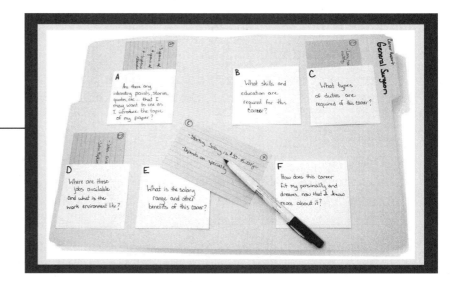

This 3-Dimensional writing tool helps keep all notes, thoughts, and memos in a logical order.

Materials Needed

- ❑ 1 file folder
- ❑ 3 or 4 envelopes (size 6: 3 ⅝ x 6 ½")
- ❑ 12-30 index cards (3 x 5")
- ❑ Glue
- ❑ Pen or marker
- ❑ Scissors
- ❑ Copy of the *Report Planning Guide* from Appendix page 120 (optional, but helpful for the first time you use this tool)

Directions for Assembly

1○

Seal the envelopes shut, then cut them in half to form pockets. You will need one pocket for each paragraph of your report.

2○

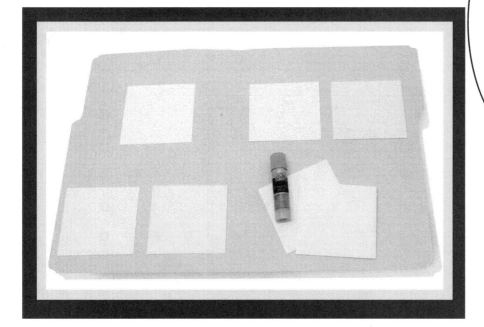

Glue the halved envelopes onto the inside surface of your file folder, as pictured. Make sure the opening of the pocket is towards the TOP of the folder.

3°

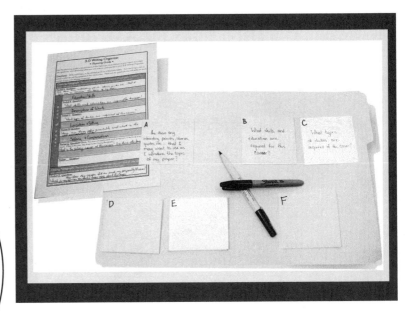

Label each pocket in alphabetic order. Use the Writing Planning Guide (on page 120) to determine the questions each paragraph will answer. Record one question on each pocket.

4°

On the front cover of your folder, list all sources you will use for your research including encyclopedias, magazines, websites, and books.

Number each source.

5∘

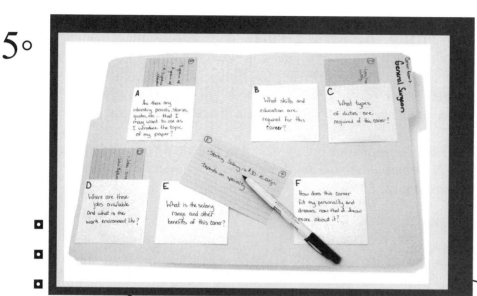

Start your research. As you find an answer for each question, record the answer on an index card.

To avoid plagiarism, write your answers in your own words and record the page number of the source from where the information was found. If you believe using a direct quote is best, be sure to put quotations around the text that you copy on your index card.

6∘

In the upper left corner of each card, record the pocket letter in which the card belongs. On the right-hand corner, write the source number for each card.

Once your research is complete, it's time to start writing. See the next page for more details on creating your paper.

Writing the First Draft

Once you have approximately 3-5 index cards for each pocket, you should have enough information to begin writing your paper. (You may not have as many notes for the opening and closing paragraph.)

The directions that follow will help you turn your notes from the 3-D Organizer into a solid, well-written paper. See a sample paper on page 81.

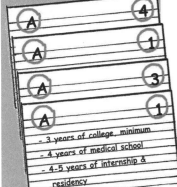

1○ Write the opening paragraph.

You may not have many (or any) notes for this paragraph because it is an overview of the paper. Sometimes, you may find that it is easier to begin the body of the paper and write the opening paragraph last. This decision may depend on your preference and/or the topic you are writing about.

2○ Check index cards from the first pocket.

Make sure they all answer the question for that specific pocket.

3○ Arrange the cards in the most logical order.

If you are having difficulty, imagine you are explaining the information to someone in a conversation. This strategy will not only help you figure out the order, but it will also help you with step 4.

4○ Write the paragraph.

Use your index cards to help you determine what to write. To make the language sound natural, use your own words as much as possible. Use the tip from Step 3 and imagine you are telling the information to someone else. This approach will help your writing transition from one detail to another without sounding like a list of facts.

5° **Repeat steps 2-4 for the remaining paragraphs.**

6° **Write a closing paragraph.**

Closing paragraphs summarize the main idea of the report and often contain a short statement about your personal thoughts, comments, or observations about the topic. The closing paragraph will often connect to a fact or comment written in the opening paragraph.

7° **Revise your paper.**

Revising involves making sure that your paper "sounds" good. Do all sentences flow together and make sense? Do the paragraphs make sense and transition nicely from one to another? Revising checklists are a nice tool to use for this phase of the writing process. It is always a good idea to ask an adult to help you revise as well.

8° **Finally, edit your paper.**

Use spell check and grammar check on the computer, but never rely on them completely. Check your own paper for misspellings, typos, correct grammar, etc. Then, ask someone else to double-check your paper for spelling and grammar, as well.

These note cards were used to write the highlighted paragraph on page 81.

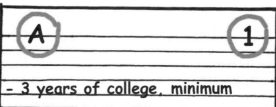

A   **1**

- 3 years of college, minimum
- 4 years of medical school
- 4-5 years of internship & residency

A   **3**

- More than 80% of medical students borrow money to cover expenses.

A   **1**

-Surgeons must be self-motivated and be able to handle pressures of long hours.

A   **2**

-Surgeons are most effective when they are patient and caring to wards their patients, so they can better communicate with them and help them recover.

General Surgeon

A surgeon not only puts her mind and hands on the job, but also her heart. In many cases, the difference between life and death rests in her hands. As a general surgeon, I would have the opportunity to help other people in a very meaningful way and would also be able to stay active, instead of sitting at a desk all day.

To become a surgeon, there is an extensive amount of education and training required. First, surgeons must complete at least three years of college. Afterwards, they are required to attend four years of medical school and then participate in an internship and residency which could take up to 5 years. The training is not cheap, either! More than 80% of medical students borrow money to cover their expenses while in school. Surgeons must be self-motivated and able to handle pressures of long hours on the job. The most effective surgeons are people who are patient and caring towards their patients. These traits allow them to communicate with their patients to help them recover better.

The nature of work that a surgeon does will depend on his/her specialty. Most surgeons will specialize in a specific area such as cardiology, orthopedics, or oncology, to name a few. Regardless of specialty, however, surgeons can usually count on long hours. Most work 60 or more hours per week in hospitals, clinics, or other private practices. These hours are often split between office consultations and the operating room.

Some of the most highly trained surgeons in the country work in the top three research and patient care facilities in the United States: John Hopkins in Baltimore, Mayo Clinic in Rochester, MN, and Massachusetts General Hospital in Boston. However, most surgeons are likely to find work in any part of the country, particularly in more urban areas. Surgeons do not typically travel for work, except when they attend out-of-town medical seminars for further training. Otherwise, the only travel surgeons take is on vacation, which is typically 20-30 vacation days per year.

All of the expenses for medical school may be worth it when you consider the salaries some surgeons make. Average salary is approximately $255,000. While starting salary is $30,000-$45,000 a year, earning potential grows rapidly. Earnings usually depend on how many patients a surgeon sees and the types of procedures she performs.

There are many pros and cons to working in the medical field. Overall, however, I think I would enjoy being able to help people, even help save lives. Despite the long hours and expensive training, I would certainly sacrifice some things to save others; I want to touch the hearts of other people in life. If I were a patient that had to undergo surgery, I would certainly want a surgeon with this level of compassion.

If you notice, each paragraph in the career research paper on the previous page answers the questions that were created on page 72. Creating questions before you write significantly helps you focus your research and keep your paragraphs on topic.

Computerized 3-D Research Report Organizer

If you have a large paper to write or simply prefer to use the computer to record your research, you can apply the concept of the file folder organizer to the computer. (This variation works particularly well for papers that are more than eight paragraphs long.) You should use the file- folder organizer at least once before using the computerized version as the previous process is a little more concrete and easy to follow for first-time use.

1° Using your word processor program, create a "New Folder" and give it the same title as your paper.

2° Create a new document within this folder for each question you will need to answer. (The computer documents will replace the envelope pockets.) The title of each document will, of course, be the question that you would have written on the pockets of your file folder.

3° Instead of filling out index cards as you do your research, you simply click on each question (document) as you find a relevant answer and type the information in the document. Make a bullet-point list of answers, indicating the source for each one.

4° When you have completed your research and are ready to write your first draft, simply print each document and use the information on each document to create your paragraphs. For longer papers, your "question documents" may represent separate sections in your paper, instead of paragraphs.

chapter 11

Taking & Studying Notes

The art of taking and studying notes is more than simply writing down information as a teacher is lecturing. It is about paying attention and really *trying* to understand what your teacher is teaching. It is about being able to identify important information so that you are not spending so much time writing down insignificant details and missing the big picture. It is being able to identify when you are lost *before* it is too late and knowing how to get clarification. Finally, it is about learning the information so you can properly recall it for a test.

Sound impossible?

It is actually fairly simple, once you understand some basic strategies for creating and using notes taken in class.

Priming Your Brain:
Developing a Purpose for Note-Taking

As it was discussed in Chapter 9, priming your brain will help new information 'stick' to it more efficiently. It is not only important to prime your brain for reading text books, but also for listening to lectures.

"How do you 'prime' your brain for a class lecture?"

Ironically, the best thing you can do to prime your brain for a class lecture is to read about the topic in your text book *before* class. (At the very least, read the pictures and visuals before class.) This strategy develops background information to help you make better sense of topics covered in class, increasing your ability to focus because you will be anticipating some of the information your teacher will be discussing. You will also be able to ask questions about things you may not have understood when you read your text book. (This is great for interacting with your teachers, too!)

If you are not able to read your text book before class, at least have your book open to related pages while your teacher is lecturing. With your text book open, you can be looking at corresponding pictures, graphs, and other information regarding what your teacher is lecturing. Not only does this help you pay attention better, it also helps you learn and remember information more quickly because you are connecting it to visual cues.

> *When you read your text before class and prime your brain while taking notes, the time needed to study for tests will instantly be cut by 50% or more.*

As your teacher is lecturing, constantly ask yourself one key question; "How does this information relate to the main topic?" This simple question will allow you to continuously create connections, which will help you make better sense of the information you are hearing.

Many of these strategies do not take any additional time, but they do *save* time because they maximize your brain's efficiency. Even though reading your text book does take some time, if you follow the steps listed in Chapter 9, you will be able to read much more quickly than you have in the past. When you read your text before class and prime your brain while taking notes, the time needed to study for tests will instantly be cut by 50% or more.

Taking Notes

In addition to 'priming' your brain, there are some more helpful tips for taking notes on the next two pages. Notice, the left 1/3 of the page is blank. This is intentional so that you have some space to record summary questions after class. The process of turning your notes into questions will allow you to process the information at a higher level of thinking (rather than just memorizing) and will create instant study guides for you as you prepare for tests. See samples of summary questions on the next three pages.

Notes on Taking Notes

Oct. 18

- **Date every page**
  - Helps determine what information will be on specific tests/quizzes.

Why date every page?
  - Keeps papers in order in the event your binder "pops" open.

- **Fold the left 1/3 of the paper**

Why fold the left 1/3 of the paper?
  - Write notes on right 2/3 of the paper.
  - Create summary questions on the left side, as demonstrated on this page. (No more than 5 questions per page).

Why create summary questions?
  - * Turning your notes into questions helps you learn information at a higher level and therefore remember it better.
  - * The questions become an instant study guide.

- **Take notes when a teacher…**
  - Says "This will be on the test." (Put a * next to it!)
  - Says "This is an important point…"
  - Writes information on the board.

Keep the back pages of the notebook paper open for adding additional information, drawing charts, pictures, symbols for your notes, etc.

Notes are easier to read and study when information is not crammed on each page. Give yourself some space to add additional information. Don't be stingy on the paper when you are taking notes...there are better ways to save trees.

Oct. 18

- Take notes when a teacher (cont.):

- Repeats the same information twice.

- Slows down as she speaks, giving you time to write.

- Talks with exaggerated hand gestures.

When should I take notes?
- Explains the same concept in several different ways.

- Says, "This is not in your text book, but it is important..."

- Other Considerations:

- When possible, draw visuals (sketches, diagrams, charts, symbols) as you take notes.

- If you miss something, draw a blank line as a place holder and clarify later.

What are some other things I can do when taking notes?
- Keep it short. Write as little as possible. Use the same abbreviations you use for texting and create a few more of your own; your notes only have to make sense to you!

- Use as much space as you need to create clear notes for yourself.

Studying Notes

Taking notes alone is not enough. You also need to know how to use your notes effectively. Some tips for efficiently studying notes are listed below. If done regularly, these steps can usually be completed in 15 minutes or less.

1 **Review all new notes within 24 hours of class.** Then, go back and briefly review *all* notes taken since the last test for each class. Reading notes immediately and repeatedly, even for just a few minutes, takes advantage of the way your brain operates. You will no longer have to labor over memorizing notes because you will solidly know the information.

2 **Record any information or visuals you remember from class but did not have time to write down.** Highlight items for which you have questions or simply do not understand. Ask your teacher about these items in class the next day.

3 **Create questions that summarize important points in your notes.** You can also think of potential exam questions that could be developed from the information in your notes.

4 **Review your notes by reading them out loud.** When you read silently, your brain only processes information through your eyes. When you read notes out loud, your brain processes information through your eyes (reading), your mouth (speaking), and your ears (hearing). This increases your brain's ability to recall information on tests.

There are additional formats for note-taking, such as concept webs (great for learning science or social studies vocabulary) and graphic organizers. Log on to www.StudySkills.com for more FREE resources.

Studying Math Notes

Many students do not understand what it means to "study" for a math test. *Studying* conjures images of reading and memorizing a lot of notes, which is usually not very practical for math. While there are occasional notes taken in math class (i.e. vocabulary terms and sample problems), most of your math notes will actually come from your homework. Studying for a math test means not only studying the vocabulary, but doing your homework regularly and paying attention to corrections made in class. It also means learning from mistakes and doing practice problems to prepare for a test.

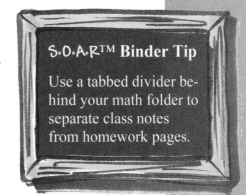

S.O.A.R™ Binder Tip

Use a tabbed divider behind your math folder to separate class notes from homework pages.

Since studying for math tests begins with doing the homework, the information on the next page will correlate with the math assignment on page 91. This assignment represents a typical piece of homework you might have to do in math. Although the types of problems may be different from your current math work, the concepts apply to nearly all forms of math assignments.

The numbers below correspond to the same symbols on the next page.

1 ALWAYS put the page number and problem numbers at the top of the page.

2 Use a new page for each new assignment and use plenty of space to NEATLY do your work. Keep place values aligned properly so that all digits in the ones place align, tens place, etc. Any math teacher will confirm that too many points are lost on math tests by students who cannot read their own writing and end up confusing themselves!

3 If you encounter a problem that you do not know how to do, RE-MAIN CALM. Look at the lesson in your book to see if you can figure out how to do the problem. If, after 5 minutes, you cannot figure it out, circle the problem number, record it at the top of the page, and MOVE ON. Continue to skip any problems that you cannot figure out and come back to them once you have completed all of the problems that you can do.

4 If you get to the end of the assignment and you only have a few problems that you cannot answer, leave them and ask your teacher about them the next day. (Make sure you have at least demonstrated that you tried the problems.)   If you cannot figure out the majority of the assignment, then you need to ask for help from your parent(s), a neighbor, your teacher, or in-school tutoring.

5 Most teachers begin math class by correcting homework from the night before and asking, "Are there any questions from last night's homework?" Make sure you raise your hand and get your questions answered (this helps build rapport with your teacher, too).

6 When it is time to prepare for a test, go back through your homework from the chapter and redo the problems with which you had trouble.

Conclusion

These simple steps help ensure that you are learning the material consistently throughout a chapter or unit, rather than cramming the night before a test (which is nearly impossible, especially in math). A few simple steps while doing your math homework will make class time more valuable, save you a lot of study time, and help you score higher grades on tests.

9-24-04

1 Pg. 26 #1-21 odd

2

1. $\begin{array}{r} 261 \\ + 33 \\ \hline 294 \end{array}$

3. $\begin{array}{r} 42\overset{1}{7} \\ + 56 \\ \hline 483 \end{array}$

5. $\begin{array}{r} 6\overset{1}{2}4 \\ + 39 \\ \hline 663 \end{array}$

7. $\begin{array}{r} \overset{8}{9}\overset{1}{7}8 \\ - 86 \\ \hline 892 \end{array}$

9. $\begin{array}{r} 1752 \\ - 40 \\ \hline 1712 \end{array}$

11. $\begin{array}{r} 20\overset{3}{4}\overset{1}{3} \\ - 38 \\ \hline 2005 \end{array}$

3 (13.) $\begin{array}{r} 30\overset{1}{8}2 \\ - 654 \\ \hline 8 \end{array}$

15. $\begin{array}{r} \overset{3}{3}4\overset{1}{0}2 \\ \times \quad 9 \\ \hline 30{,}618 \end{array}$

(17.) $\begin{array}{r} \overset{6}{3}\overset{4}{9}\overset{3}{6}5 \\ \times \quad 27 \\ \hline 27755 \\ 0 \end{array}$

(19.) $\begin{array}{r} 4861 \\ \times \quad 25 \\ \hline 24305 \\ 20 \end{array}$

4

This assignment may not reflect the same level of math that you are currently studying, but these concepts will apply to most math assignments.

chapter 12

Taking Tests

❑ **Do you ever get nervous when taking a test?**

❑ **Does the thought of studying for tests ever feel overwhelming?**

❑ **Have you ever been disappointed with your score on a test after you worked hard to prepare for it?**

❑ **Do you ever feel like there *has* to be a better way to prepare for and perform on tests?**

There *is* a better way…

As with everything else, there are a few tricks and tips for making test preparation and test-taking more efficient.

The test on the next two pages will assess your test-taking I.Q. and give you some cues about good strategies to use. Try the test first, then read the Answer Key, beginning on page 95, to correct your answers and identify hidden clues within each question.

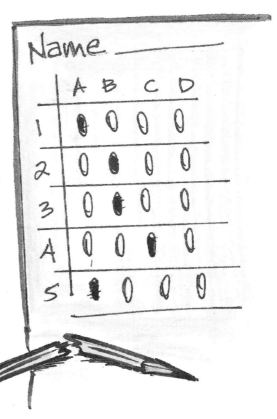

The Test Test

▀▄▀▄▀▄▀▄▀

<u>Directions:</u> At the end of each statement, write True or False in the blank line. Ignore the "correct statement" line until after you have read the answer key.

① Most of your test-preparation is done when you take notes, read the text, and develop questions about both. _____

Correct statement:

_____
_____

② You should throw away all of your work as soon as it is checked or graded because it will only clutter up your folders. _____

Correct statement:

_____
_____

③ Getting a good night's sleep and eating a healthy breakfast are more beneficial than cramming all night the night before a test. _____

Correct statement:

_____
_____

④ When you are undecided about a test answer, your first hunch is usually right. _____

Correct statement:

_____
_____

⑤ It is important to be the first person done with the test because that means that you aced the test. _____

Correct statement:

_____
_____

Continue ➜

The Test Test

Multiple choice: Underline the best answer for each question.

⑥ The best way to study for a test is:

    A. Spend a few solid hours of non-stop studying the night before a test.

    B. Do your reading and homework on time and review your notes for a few minutes everyday.

    C. Highlight any questions that you have on any of your work or notes so that you remember to ask them in class.

    D. Both B and C.

⑦ Preparing a study-guide…

    A. Should be based only on what the teacher tells you about the test.

    B. Is automatically done for you when you use the questioning technique for taking notes and reading.

    C. Means spending many hours, the night before the test, rewriting all of your notes.

    D. Only needs to be done for big tests, such as final exams.

⑧ When your teacher gives you a study guide, you should:

    A. Ignore it because you have already made your own study guide from your notes.

    B. Use it to help you decipher what to focus on the night or two before the test.

    C. Toss your notes and text book aside; the study guide is all you need.

    D. Stop paying attention in class. The study guide has all the answers you will need for the test.

⑨ The night before a test, you should:

    A. Look over your work for a minute. You don't need to spend any more time on it because you've taken notes and done your homework.

    B. Spend a few solid hours studying non-stop.

    C. Spend 30-60 minutes reviewing your notes, homework, and text, and quizzing yourself by talking out-loud.

    D. None of the above.

⑩ To study for a final exam or unit test, your best option is to:

    A. Study corrected tests from the semester.

    B. Reread every chapter covered since the beginning of the semester.

    C. Forget studying. You either know it or you don't.

    D. None of the above.

STOP ●

The Test Test

⬛ANSWER KEY⬛

Now that you have completed the test, check your answers below and find additional hints for taking tests.

Directions: At the end of each statement, write True or False in the blank line. Ignore the "correct statement" line until after you have read the answer key.

Did you notice the statement in the directions that told you to *ignore* the "correct statement line" until after you read the answer key?

An average of 50% of students taking any given test do not read the directions. If this was a real test and you did not follow these directions, you could have lost points already.

Lesson: Pay attention to the directions!

① Most of your test-preparation is done when you take notes, read the text, and develop questions about both. **TRUE**

Hint:

The word "most" is an indication that this answer is probably true. Anytime a T/F question has a word such as "some," "most," "few," etc. the answer is probably true. Conversely, most questions that have words like "all" or "none" are likely to be false because very few things are that definitive.

② You should throw away all of your work as soon as it is checked or graded because it will only clutter up your folders. **FALSE**

Correct Statement:

Old assignments, especially old tests/quizzes, are the most valuable study guides you can have for final exams or unit tests. Do not throw anything away until you have received your final grade in case your teacher made a computational mistake. If your binder is getting overloaded, transfer papers to your home filing system.

③ Getting a good night's sleep and eating a healthy breakfast are more beneficial than cramming all night the night before a test. **TRUE**

Hint:

Good sleep and proper nutrition will keep you alert and help prevent "stupid" mistakes. In fact, drowsy drivers have been shown to demonstrate similar behavior on the road as some drunk drivers, illustrating how impaired your thinking and reasoning can be when you are tired.

④ When you are undecided about a test answer, your first hunch is usually right.   **TRUE**

Hint:

If you are truly stuck and have no clue about an answer, go with whatever answer first seemed most appropriate to you. Chances are that your subconscious, long-term memory is working on your behalf, but is simply lacking the proper recall to help you clarify the answer.

⑤ It is important to be one of the first people done with the test because that means that you aced the test. **FALSE**

Correct Statement:

There is no such thing as a stupid question, but there is such a thing as a *stupid* answer; those are the items that, after your test has been graded, make you think, "OHHH! I knew that!" The best way to avoid *stupid* mistakes is to take the time to reread your test when you are done. Use all the time you have. It is a little frustrating trying to concentrate after you have completed the test, but EVERY POINT COUNTS. If you reread your tests regularly, you will likely find and correct an error more than 50% of the time!

Multiple choice: Underline the best answer for each question.

Did you notice that the instructions told you to underline the answer? Little details in the directions like this are commonly overlooked by students. Sometimes, these omissions can cost points from the final score.

⑥ The best way to study for a test is:

    A. Spend a few solid hours of non-stop studying the night before a test.

    B. Do your reading and homework on time and review your notes for a few minutes everyday.

    C. Highlight any questions that you have on any of your work or notes so that you remember to ask them in class.

    D. <u>Both B and C.</u>

Hint:

Teachers like to cram a lot of information into questions. Anytime you see more than one option combined together, such as "All of the above," or "Both B & C," that answer is *likely* to be correct.

⑦ Preparing a study-guide…

    A. Should be based only on what the teacher tells you about the test.

    B. <u>Is automatically done for you when you use the questioning technique for taking notes and reading text books.</u>

    C. Means spending many hours, the night before the test, rewriting all of your notes.

    D. Only needs to be done for big tests, such as final exams.

Hint:

If you have no other clue to figure out an answer, then choose the longest answer…it is usually the correct choice.

⑧ When your teacher gives you a study guide, you should:

    A. Ignore it because you have already made your own study guide from your notes.

    B. <u>Use it to help you decipher what to focus on the night or two before the test.</u>

    C. Toss your notes and text book aside; the study guide is all you need.

    D. Stop paying attention in class. The study guide has all the answers you will need for the test.

Hint:

If possible, avoid being absent the day or two before a test. Valuable test information is usually given at this time.

⑨ The night before a test, you should:
   A. Look over your work for a minute. You don't need to spend any more time on it because you've taken notes and done your homework.
   B. Spend a few solid hours studying non-stop.
   C. <u>Spend 30-60 minutes reviewing your notes, homework, and text book, then quiz yourself by talking out-loud</u>.
   D. None of the above.

Hint:

If you have consistently been doing homework and reviewing notes, then 30-60 minutes reviewing and making final connections the night before a test should be all you need. This preparation will also give you valuable confidence before a test.

⑩ To study for a final exam or unit test, your best option is to:
   A. <u>Study corrected tests from the semester</u>.
   B. Reread every chapter covered since the beginning of the semester.
   C. Forget studying. You either know it or you don't.
   D. None of the above.

Hint:

Who has time for "B"? The answer is clearly "A" because teachers do not have a lot of time to create brand new questions for end-of-semester (or end-of-unit) tests. Therefore, they usually pull questions from previous tests and quizzes for their final exams.

Your Score:
_____ out of 10

If you scored:

- **9-10**…Congratulations, you are a test-taking champ!

- **6-8**… You have a good start. Practice a couple of the strategies in this chapter to improve your test performance.

- **1-5**… Reread the chapter and select three-four strategies you can begin practicing right away. In a month, try two more.

More Test-Taking Tips

It cannot be emphasized enough…the single best way to perform well on tests is to study notes and information for a few minutes everyday, keep up with your homework, and read assigned text book pages. (At the very least, read the pictures!) When you do each of these things, you are guaranteed a solid performance on tests. However, there are some other tips to consider:

A⁺ **Have a watch or clock available when taking a test.** Proper pacing is important when taking a test. Before you even see the test, ask your teacher how much time you will have and how many questions will be on the test. (This is a good question to ask the day before the test.)

A⁺ **Before you do anything else, do an overview of the entire test by quickly reading each question.** There are two benefits to this:

    1) You will have a picture of the whole test and will be better able to judge how much time to spend on each question or section.

    2) Many times, clues for some answers are included in other questions. By reviewing the test before you start, you may find a few answers.

A⁺ **If you get to a question that you don't know, don't waste your time and energy; mark the question, skip it, and move on.** Otherwise, you are likely to waste a lot of time and build up anxiety that could cause you to lose focus on the rest of the test. Don't forget, however, to go back to that question after you complete the rest of the test.

A⁺ **When you first receive a test, immediately write down any information you needed to memorize, such as formulas, specific dates, names, etc.** Write this information down right away to keep from getting anxious or flustered and forgetting important information.

Multiple Choice Questions

A⁺ After reading the question, try to think of the correct answer BEFORE you read your options.

A⁺ Read all answers first. Sometimes, item "A" will *sound* correct, but item "C" may end up being more appropriate.

A⁺ Cross out items that you know are wrong and then choose your answer from the remaining options.

A⁺ Answers with phrases like "all of the above" and "both a & b" are likely to be the correct choices, but only use this clue if you are stuck.

A⁺ The longest answers are also likely to be the correct choices, but again, only use this clue if you do not have any other ideas.

Fill-in-the-Blank Questions

A⁺ Look for grammar clues that may give hints, such as the word "an" that will indicate that the answer begins with a vowel, or something that indicates a plural word, past tense verb, etc.

A⁺ Sometimes the length and/or number of blanks may be a hint.

A⁺ After you have filled in the blank, reread the statement with your answer to make sure that your answer makes sense in the sentence.

Essay Questions

A⁺ In the margin, write a brief outline of the major points you want to include in your answer. This will help you write an organized, logical, and concise answer. Teachers do not want to read lengthy responses. They prefer short and to-the-point answers. In fact, many teachers may *only* read your outline when grading your paper. An outline may also help you get partial credit if you run out of time.

A⁺ Begin your answer by restating the question. Remember, get to the point quickly.

A⁺ Write neatly. It is definitely NOT to your advantage to frustrate your teacher!

Conclusion

This chapter includes several tips for improving performance on tests. However, the single best way to prepare for tests is to read your text books, regularly review notes, and learn from your homework assignments and quizzes. Following these steps will ensure that you have a solid grasp of the information and will have no problems acing any test!

Ask questions
-Summary-

1   **Having your teachers' support can benefit you and your grades in many ways.** Most teachers see 100-150 students every day. They need you to let them know that you are diligent about your schoolwork by asking questions and participating in class.

2   **You can improve your reading speed and comprehension by "priming your brain" before you read.** To encourage the information you read to 'stick,' ask yourself a variety of questions before you begin reading.

3   **Questions can help you write papers, too.** Use questions to help you identify key information that your paper should address. These questions can then be transformed into starter sentences for paragraphs and help you organize your information.

4   **Questions also prime your brain for taking and studying notes.** The more prepared you are for class, the more you will be able to focus, identify important information to write down, and increase your retention. Questions also help you create a study guide out of your notes.

5   **The best way to prepare for tests is to consistently ask questions throughout a chapter or unit of study.** Creating questions out of the information helps your brain make the connections that are so important for recall.

Record your progress

section 5

Record your progress

Check all statements below that apply to you:

_____ I am sometimes shocked, and occasionally disappointed, by the grades I see on my report card.

_____ I always have good intentions of doing better in school, but I sometimes lose track of my goals.

_____ I have learned a lot of good information in this program, I'm just not sure where to start.

You will find solutions to these problems, and much more, in the following section.

Spend more time examining *yourself*, and less time seeking the approval of others.

In a television interview, First Lady Laura Bush was once asked if she had a message to share with her twin daughters as they graduated from college. Mrs. Bush indicated that she wanted her daughters to pursue their passions and interests. More importantly, however, she said she wanted them to know the value of hard work and the deep feeling of satisfaction that comes from applying oneself and achieving a goal.

> *"Nobody can talk you into feeling good about yourself. You get that solid good feeling from success."*
>
> - Dr. David K. Reynolds

Dr. David K. Reynolds would agree with Mrs. Bush. Dr. Reynolds is a psychologist that teaches a unique, but powerful approach to developing self-esteem. Like Mrs. Bush, he believes that **taking action** is the one true way to develop a positive feeling about yourself and to develop a positive attitude towards life. As he says, "Nobody can talk you into feeling good about yourself-you get that solid good feeling from success." Of course, success does not come free, but it is so incredibly rewarding!

Recording your progress is an essential piece in pulling the S·O·A·R™ Study Skills System together and ensuring that you will achieve success. The process of recording your grades and goals will help keep you focused, on track, and motivated. It will also help you recognize your accomplishments and attain that remarkable feeling of success!

chapter 13
Tracking Your Grades

"Why should *I* keep track of my own grades?"

If you have ever been surprised by a grade on your report card, you already know one reason why you should keep track of your own grades. Often, when students receive a 'bad' grade, they have a tendency to blame their teachers. But, your teacher does not *invent* your grade...you *earn* it. While teachers offer assistance and may offer a point or two to boost your grade, 99.9% of the work rests on your shoulders. Keeping track of your own grades helps you see exactly how you earn your grade; what scores give your grade a boost and what scores send you falling.

Tracking your own grades improves your grades! That's right, the process of tracking your scores allows you to see exactly how each point affects your grade. This knowledge will help you stay motivated about turning homework in on time, being a little more careful when answering test questions, etc. Unfortunately, low scores on one or two assignments can lower your grade fast. While it's not impossible to pull your grade back up, it can be difficult. It is far better to be proactive and prevent the slippery slope from starting.

When you keep track of your own grades, you can catch any mistakes your teacher may have made. (It happens more often than you might think.) Have you ever seen the tiny boxes in which teachers have to record grades for each student? It is very easy to put the wrong grade in a slot, or perhaps simply record the number incorrectly. You can help your teacher stay accurate by recording your own grades, too. One note of caution… If you think your teacher has made an error, be *very* polite about it! Say something like, "Mrs. Smith, I think there may be a problem with my grade." rather than, "Mrs. Smith, YOU made a mistake!" Do you see the difference?

Calculating your grades can sometimes save you work. You can often calculate the score you need on an upcoming test in order to receive a specific final grade. You can use this information to determine how much time you should spend studying. For example, I once figured out that it did not matter if I earned an "A" or a "F" on my French final exam because I would still get a "B" for my final grade. So, I used my time to study for other subjects. (As it turns out, I did so poorly on the final exam that my teacher actually called me at home to reassure me that I would still get a "B" on my report card. She was afraid I might be worrying about it. At least I was able to do much better on all of my other exams!)

To summarize, tracking your own grades will allow you to:

- ☑ Avoid surprises on your report card.

- ☑ See how each assignment and every point can affect your grade.

- ☑ Gain a sense of control over your grades.

- ☑ Keep track of your teacher's records…they can make mistakes, too!

- ☑ Set more accurate goals for each test and assignment.

"How do I keep track of my own grades?"

Many school systems utilize some type of web-based system that allows students to look up their grades on-line throughout each marking period. If you have that service available, use it and check it regularly! Watch how your scores on assignments and tests affect your grade, check to make sure the scores you see on-line match the scores you earned, and use the information to set some goals for upcoming tests and projects.

If your school does not offer such a service, you can use the simple tracking sheet on page 109 to keep track of your grades. (See directions on the next page.) It does take a little bit of time, but recording and calculating your grades is a good thing to do during those first few minutes of class while you are waiting for the bell to ring and for things to get started.

Calculating Your Grades

<u>Directions</u>: Use the table below to see how to keep track of your grades throughout a marking period. Refer to the steps that follow for a specific explanation.

Date	Assignment	# of points / # of points possible	Total # of points / Total points poss.	Percentage
9-10	Homework #1	$\frac{9}{10}$	$\frac{9}{10}$	90%
9-16	Homework #2	$\frac{8}{10}$	$\frac{9}{10} + \frac{8}{10} = \frac{17}{20}$	85%
9-30	Quiz #1	$\frac{20}{30}$	$\frac{17}{20} + \frac{20}{30} = \frac{37}{50}$	74%
10-8	Test #1	$\frac{50}{50}$	$\frac{37}{50} + \frac{50}{50} = \frac{87}{100}$	87%

Step 1:

Record each of your graded assignments as they are returned to you.

Step 2:

In the third column, you will write a fraction for the number of points you scored out of points possible for that assignment. In the shaded column, you will keep a running record of your grade by adding the new assignment points to the total points earned in the class up to that point. For example, this student scored 9 out of 10 points on Homework #1 and 8 out of 10 points on Homework #2. His total points possible after his 2nd homework assignment are 17 out of 20.

Step 3:

Use a calculator to calculate your current percentage score. You can figure this out by dividing your total points earned out of total points possible. You will get a decimal. Multiply this decimal by 100 for your percent score (points earned / points possible x 100 = _____%).

Helpful Hint

Make copies of the form on the next page and place one copy in the front of each folder in your binder. As you get papers back, record the grades on your Tracking Sheet, and place the corrected assignments behind it.

Grade Tracking Sheet

Name: _____

Class: _____ Marking Period: _____

Date	Assignment	# of points # of points possible	Total # of points Total points poss.	Percentage

❑ Make one copy of this page for every class and put one in each folder in your binder.
❑ Record your grades as assignments are passed back.
❑ Replace this Tracking Sheet at each new Marking Period.

www.StudySkills.com

Chapter 14
Monitoring Your Goals

There are many different type of goals: long-term career goals, things you would like to do sometime in your lifetime, things you would like to accomplish within a year, things you hope to do tomorrow, etc. All of these goals are an important part of inspiring you to achieve good grades; When you have something to look forward to, it is much easier to stay motivated.

For the purposes of this program, we will focus on two types of goals: your long-term goals for each marking period, and your short-term goals for each week.

Beginning of Each Marking Period

Earlier in this book, you spent some time analyzing your goals for the next marking period. It is important to do this at the beginning of each semester when you have a clean slate and can have a fresh start! Make a copy of the goal sheet on page 111 and post it somewhere where you will see it often: on the wall or a bulletin board in your room, the front pocket of your binder, even on the wall in your bathroom where you will see it every morning. The important thing is to put it in a place where you will see it often and consistently be reminded of what you want to achieve.

Goals I will accomplish...

In order to achieve a healthy balance in your life, create a long-term goal for school, for your health, and for something outside of school. Reevaluate these goals at the beginning of each quarter/semester.

Remember the key to achieving your goals is to TAKE ACTION!

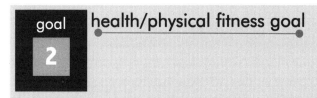

goal 1 school goal

goal 2 health/physical fitness goal

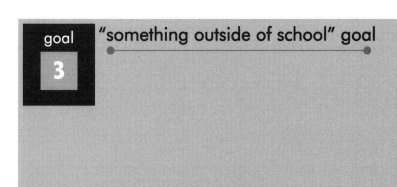

goal 3 "something outside of school" goal

Post this page someplace where you will see it everyday.
Use these long-term goals to help you determine your weekly goals.

Beginning of Each Week

The path toward reaching your long-term goals is paved with small action steps. The best way to take these steps is to get each week off to a good start with a little bit of planning. At the beginning of the week (just before you talk to your parents about each of your schedules), review your planner to see what you have coming up the following week:

☐ Record test and project dates in your planner for the week (if you have not already done so).

☐ Set three goals for yourself for the week. (See *Weekly Goals* on the sample planner sheet on the next page.)

☐ Think about when you can take action to accomplish those goals and map them out in your planner.

Now that you have come to the end of the SOAR™ Study Skills Program and have learned many other strategies, it is appropriate to take another look at the sample planner page we saw in Section Two. Do you see how weekly planning automatically develops the routine of monitoring your goals? A few minutes at the beginning of each week is all you need to revisit your goals and continue to plan how you will achieve them.

Flexibility Is Key

It is important to acknowledge that, inevitably, your week will not turn out exactly as you plan. Sometimes you may have 1 or 2 days that fall off course, and other times it may be the whole week. When this happens, don't give up on your goals, but rely on your ability to make decisions according to your priorities, then try to get back on track as soon as possible. It may occasionally be a few weeks before you resume the habit of weekly planning...that's normal. Just don't give up on it permanently.

Conclusion

It may seem like this chapter is a repeat of concepts covered in Section Two. In a way, it is. The point is to illustrate that the process of setting, tracking, and achieving goals is not a one-time thing, but an ongoing and cyclical process. Your goals will naturally grow and change over time, so it is important to develop the habit of reevaluating and planning for them on a regular basis.

Sept	3 Monday	4 Tuesday	5 Wednesday	6 Thursday	7 Friday	8 Saturday
1st hour	Page 161 # 2-20 all					- *Get homework done this morning (2 hours?)*
2nd hour	None					
3rd hour	Get Permission Slip Signed					
4th hour	None					
5th hour						
6th hour	Study for Chapter 4 Test on Thurs.					**9 Sunday**
7th hour	Read section 5.2. Questions pg. 109			Science test today		*Grandma's b-day* lunch 1 p.m.
Other	Math book Science book Language Arts book					
3 p.m.	Snack	Movie Club Mtg. Snack	Snack	Snack	Snack	**Weekly Goals**
4 p.m.	Shoot hoops & run	Shoot hoops & run	Review all notes for 15 minutes/ Do Math	Shoot hoops & run	Review all notes for 15 minutes	– Shoot hoops and run three days this week
5 p.m.	Review all notes for 15 minutes/ Do Math	Review all notes for 15 minutes/ Do Math	Study 15 min. for Science test	Review all notes for 15 minutes/ Do Math	No other homework tonight!	
6 p.m.	Study Science 15 min. L. Arts HW (1 hr)	Study 20 min. for Science test				– Review notes everyday
7 p.m.					Football game	
8 p.m.	Watch TV Show at 8:30					– Have at least two hours of homework-free time every evening!
9-10 p.m.	10:30 Read in bed/Sleep	10:30 Read in bed/Sleep	10:30 Read in bed/Sleep	10:30 Read in bed/ Sleep		

chapter 15

Recognizing Your Achievements

There is nothing like the satisfaction of accomplishing something you have worked hard to achieve. However, as human beings, we naturally notice and focus on negative things much more so than positive, which means it easy to get discouraged when you encounter setbacks. Therefore, you must make it a point to counteract your negative thoughts and acknowledge every little achievement along the way towards achieving your goals.

At the end of each day, take a moment to think about the positive things you accomplished. If you had a bad day and cannot identify even one token of success, ask yourself, "What did I *learn* from my experiences today?" This reflection is a great way to maintain a positive attitude, even during very difficult times.

In addition, at the end of each week, take a second to look back on the week and make note of the progress you made, even if it was a small fraction of what you planned. Taking this time will help you to stay motivated and will encourage you to develop skills and attitudes that will help you achieve success throughout your life.

It is impossible to undertake all of the strategies in this book at the same time; you have to take baby steps with a few ideas that fit you and your needs best. After you have experienced success with one or two techniques, you will naturally be intrigued to try more. I encourage you to revisit this book often and enjoy the process of making school-work -and life- easier for you.

□ □ □ □ □

There used to be a public service commercial targeted to smokers who were struggling to kick the habit; it encouraged them by saying, "Don't quit quitting!" In the world of SOAR™ Study Skills, the message for you is, "Don't quit **S**etting goals. Don't quit **O**rganizing. Don't quit **A**sking questions…." you get the idea!

In the meantime, take a few moments to think back to the information you have learned from this program and select the top three things you would like to try within the next month. Record them on the next page and begin immediately! Good luck!

After you hit the homerun...

...you still have to run the bases.

Congratulations! You hit a 'homerun' by completing the SOAR™ Study Skills Program. However, your efforts will not *count* unless you make the effort to try some of the new things you've learned (run the bases). In the spaces below, describe three things from this program that you will do to improve your level of success.

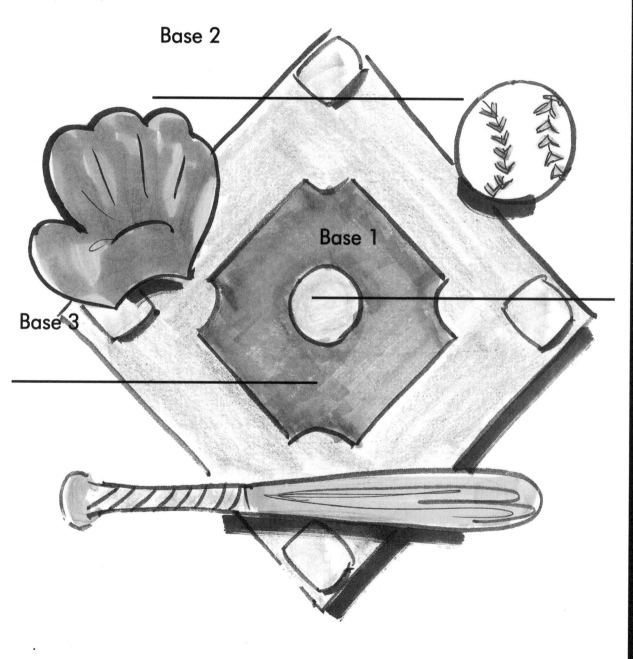

Reproducible pages referenced throughout the book are compiled in the appendix for convenient use:

appendix

Directions: This photo is for use with the activity in Chapter 9.

Look at it for no more than 5 seconds!

Now turn to page 67!

Sept	Monday	Tuesday	Wednesday	Thursday	Friday	Saturday	Sunday	Weekly Goals
1st hour								
2nd hour								
3rd hour								
4th hour								
5th hour								
6th hour								
7th hour								
Other								
3 p.m.								
4 p.m.								
5 p.m.								
6 p.m.								
7 p.m.								
8 p.m.								
9 -10 p.m.								

www.StudySkills.com

3-D Writing Organizer
◆ Planning Guide ◆

Use this planning guide to record each of the topics you must address in your report, turn them into questions, and determine what you will write on each pocket in your 3-D Writing Organizer.

<u>Directions:</u> Write each topic in the shaded portions of the table below. Turn each topic into a question and record the question in the blank rows. These are the questions you will write on each pocket of your 3-D Writing Organizer.

Opening Paragraph: The opening paragraph in most papers should capture readers' interest and give a brief overview about the topic that will be discussed in the paper.
<u>Pocket A Question:</u>

B o d y of P a p e r	
	Topic: _____
	<u>Pocket B Question:</u>
	Topic: _____
	<u>Pocket C Question:</u>
	Topic: _____
	<u>Pocket D Question:</u>
	Topic: _____
	<u>Pocket __ Question:</u> (Note: You may not need to write more paragraphs in the body of your paper. If that is the case, skip down to the Closing Paragraph.)
	Topic: _____
	<u>Pocket __ Question:</u>

Closing Paragraph: The closing paragraph summarizes the main idea of your paper and many times will include a brief personal statement about the topic.
<u>Pocket __ Question:</u>

Grade Tracking Sheet

Name:_____

Class:_____ Marking Period:_____

Date	Assignment	# of points --- # of points possible	Total # of points --- Total points poss.	Percentage

❑ Make one copy of this page for every class and put one in each folder in your binder.
❑ Record your grades as assignments are passed back.
❑ Replace this Tracking Sheet at each new Marking Period.

Goals I will accomplish...

In order to achieve a healthy balance in your life, create a long-term goal for school, for your health, and for something outside of school. Reevaluate these goals at the beginning of each quarter/semester.

Remember the key to achieving your goals is to TAKE ACTION!

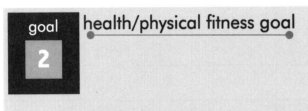

goal 1 school goal

goal 2 health/physical fitness goal

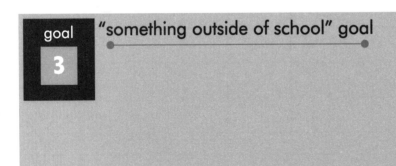

goal 3 "something outside of school" goal

Post this page someplace where you will see it everyday.
Use these long-term goals to help you determine your weekly goals.

<u>Directions</u>: These questions are for use with the activity in Chapter 9.

① What is centered directly above the man's head?

② What toy is directly above his left shoulder (on the right side of the photo)?

③ Was the snake hanging over his head striped or spotted?

④ How many times is the word "light" visible in this photo?

⑤ How many fish are in the package on the right side of the picture?

<u>Answers</u>:
① Sling shot
② *Pirate Collection*
③ spotted
④ three
⑤ four

Notes

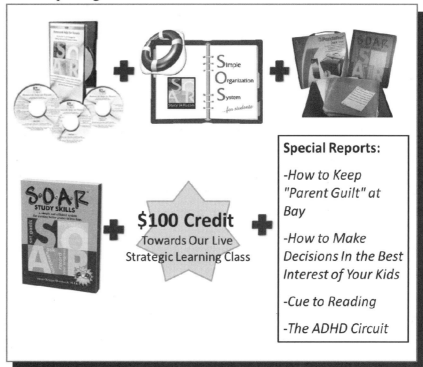

The Cost of NOT Teaching Study Skills

As school budgets are rapidly shrinking, administrators have to carefully consider how to allocate their budget; they need to get the most "bang for their buck." Managing a school budget is an art form involving hundreds of decisions and balancing dozens of demands.

HOW CAN WE MAKE THE GREATEST IMPACT?

This question is usually the first consideration and a logical place to start. To answer this question, we must consider the final objective.

Most people agree that the purpose of education is to help young people develop the skills they need to be independent, self-sufficient members of society. Of course, we also hope to arm them with skills for achieving their own sense of personal happiness and success.

HOW DO WE DO THAT?

We can look at what employers need. In 2008, a large survey of employers in "emerging sectors" were asked what skills they needed most from their employees…now, and in the future. These employers represented fields that are expected to grow significantly in the next 30 years, such as healthcare and technology.

EMPLOYERS LISTED THE TOP 57 SKILLS THEY NEED. ONLY 4 RELATED TO TECHNOLOGY!

The remaining skills were things like:

- Reading comprehension
- Critical thinking
- Active learning
- Written expression
- Time management
- Organization
- Active listening
- Attention to detail
- Learning strategies
- Independence

TABLE 4: Rank Order of Skills Spanning All Sectors

TIER 1		TIER 2	
Reading Comprehension	474	Self Control	224
Critical Thinking	461	Time Management	216
Active Learning	453	Achievement/Effort	212
Problem Sensitivity	451	Design	206
English Language	444	Stress Tolerance	206
Active Listening	444	Speech Recognition	205
Attention to Detail	432	Customer and Personal Service	194
Dependability	432	Development environment software	189
Oral Expression	421	Speaking	172
Mathematics	406	Coordination	164
Deductive Reasoning	404	Desktop computers	164
Integrity	397	Administration and Management	161
Cooperation	393	Leadership	155
Written Comprehension	377	Database mgmt system software	152
Inductive Reasoning	375		
Analytical Thinking	370		
Speech Clarity	353		
Complex Problem Solving	338		
Persistence	338		
Adaptability/Flexibility	329		
Initiative	322		
Intercultural Awareness	316		
Intercultural Sensitivity	313		
Information Ordering	308		
Near Vision	298		
Intercultural Competence	296		
Independence	293		
Intercultural Intelligence	262		
Judgment and Decision Making	260		
Engineering and Technology	252		
Troubleshooting	243		

…these are "soft skills" and they represent 95% of the top desired skills in the workplace!

The importance of "soft skills" are further supported by a study from the Stanford Research Institute and Carnegie Melon Foundation.

After surveying 500 CEOs, they determined that **75% of long-term career success depends on soft skills, while only 25% percent depends on technical knowledge.**

WHAT ARE "SOFT SKILLS?"

Soft skills are the skills needed to be a life-long learner, think critically, and make decisions independently. The skills needed to communicate effectively. They are the skills needed for a global economy!

Continued…

No matter how much more "advanced" our society gets, soft skills will always be the key to success because they allow people to effectively learn the "hard skills," or technical information, as jobs evolve.

Yet, they are largely ignored in education! On a recent internet search of "soft skills," I combed through the first 60 results before I found one link to any type of educational institution that is addressing "soft skills" in their curriculum…and it was a community college! (Delaware Tech & Community College, if you are wondering.)

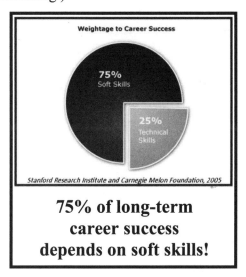

Weightage to Career Success

75% Soft Skills

25% Technical Skills

Stanford Research Institute and Carnegie Melon Foundation, 2005

75% of long-term career success depends on soft skills!

The first 59 links were mostly newspaper and magazine articles about how desperate the workplace is for these skills. You don't have to look far to see there is a great divide between the content schools are teaching and the skills needed to stay competitive in the 21st century.

We have already lost millions of jobs to other countries and the hemorrhaging will continue if we cannot right the ship. As a parent, I am arming my children with these skills because it is clear they are the key to their future success. I am personally frustrated that they do not learn _how_ to learn, process information, or have an opportunity to exercise their critical thinking skills while in school.

EDUCATION STATISTICS SUPPORT THIS CONCERN:

- **30%** of US high school students drop out of school.

- **40%** of US college students must take at least one remedial course.

- **50%** of US college students drop out before completing a degree.

- **66%** of US high school honor students fall behind in college.

DO "SOFT SKILLS" MAKE A DIFFERENCE IN SCHOOL?

"Soft skills" are synonymous with "study skills" and research shows that study skills have a big impact on school performance!

In April, 2009, Ohio State University published a study confirming the dramatic impact study skills can have on college graduation rates.

According to the study:

45% was the increased likelihood that "struggling" high school students would graduate from college if they took a study skills class.

600% was the increased likelihood that "average" high school students would graduate from college if they took a study skills class!

Imagine the impact these skills would have on students if they could learn them earlier than college?

Imagine what these skills will do for these students after college?

Continued...

Continued from previous page…

THE COST OF TEACHING EVERYTHING ELSE

Where can you make the most impact with your time and money?

 Will it be in one subject area that is narrowly focused?

Or, will it be on teaching skills that impact all subject areas, improve student performance, and actually prepare them for the workplace?

You can do the math…

The Cost of Core Subjects vs. Study Skills

Subject	Average Cost Per Student*
Math	$76.92
Language Arts	$78.48
Science	$88.29
Social Studies	$83.29
All Core Subjects	$81.75
SOAR® Study Skills	$16.99

It is 79% less expensive to teach Study Skills… and they apply across *all* content areas!

*Core subject prices are based on average price of student texts from three major publishers (educator pricing) – August 2011.

Ask the Author...

Do you have any questions about study skills? About SOAR®?

You are welcome to call us!

We are dedicated to making life easier for all of the parents, educators, and students with whom we work. That means that a live person will answer your call during office hours and we will help you right away. (In the rare event that you have to leave a message, we'll call you right back!)

We also host "Ask the Author" sessions once a month. Call to schedule a 15-minute appointment on our next "Ask the Author" afternoon. There is no charge or obligation of any kind.

This is a great opportunity for you to ask Susan any questions about study skills, implementation of SOAR®, or simply ask general questions about learning and education. We look forward to hearing from you…**You can reach us at: 800-390-SOAR.**

Curriculum Supplements

for

- Middle School
- High School
- Learning Disabilities

Regardless **if students are in 6th grade or seniors in college, the type of academic tasks they have to do are essentially the same.** Therefore, the strategies in SOAR® are appropriate for students across a wide range of grade-levels and ability levels.

However, students of various ages and abilities have unique needs. We wanted to address these needs. But, we did not want to create multiple editions and "water down" our simple and solid strategies. So, we created another solution…

SOAR® Curriculum Supplements! This companion resource provides tips and strategies for students in middle school, high school, and students with learning disabilities.

Resources Include:

✓ **Pacing guidelines for instruction.**
(Including access to a video covering helpful pacing considerations.)

✓ **The best strategies in the** *Multi-Media Teacher's Guide* for middle school, high school, and students with learning disabilities.

✓ **Schedule templates:** Pick a schedule, plug in activities from SOAR®, and your lesson planning is done!

✓ **...and more!**

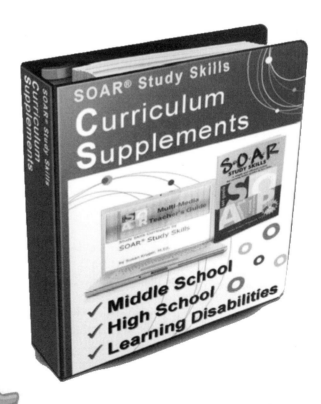

FREE

A $299 value...FREE with purchase of Curriculum from StudySkills.com!

(Minimum one *Multi-Media Teacher's Guide* & 30 books, or equivalent purchase.)

To Place an Order...

Call: 800.390.SOAR or 248.98.STUDY

Email: orders@StudySkills.com

Mail: SOAR® Learning, Inc.
2640 Canoe Circle Parkway #225
Lake Orion, MI 48360-1887

Web: www.StudySkills.com

Fax: 888.676.8481

Order Form - Page 1 of 2

Product	Product Description	Price Each		Quantity	Total
	SOAR® Study Skills Book	1-3 books: 4-20 books: 21-49 books: 50-199 books: 200-499 books: 500-1499 books: 1500 + books:	$24.99 each $19.99 each $18.50 each $17.50 each $16.99 each $15.75 each $14.99 each		*
	SOAR® Study Skills Multi-Media Teacher's Guide	$499.00			
	SOAR® Study Skills for Elementary (K-5): Parent Presentation	$299.00			
	SOAR® Study Skills for Middle & High School (6-12): Parent Presentation	$299.00			
	SOAR® Study Skills for Primary (K-2): Teacher Training Video	$299.00			*
	SOAR® Study Skills for Intermediate (3-5): Teacher Training Video	$299.00			*
	Teaching Writing (K-5): Efficient & Effective Strategies for Time-Strapped Teachers	$299.00			
	SOAR® Study Skills Tutoring Enrichment Guide	$299.00			
	SOAR® Study Skills for Middle & High School (6-12): Teacher Training Video	$299.00			

Continued on next page...

Product	Product Description	Price Each	Quantity	Total
	SOAR® Professional Development	Prices vary. Please contact us for information.		
	SOAR® Homework Help! For Parents Audio CDs	$74.99		*
	SOAR® Live Strategic Learning Classes for Students	Please visit our website to sign up www.soarSS.com/soarSLC		*
	SOAR® Organizational Supply Kit	$49.99		*

Subtotal			
Shipping *Only items marked with an asterisk in the total column require shipping.		$0.75 per item; minimum $5.00	
Sales Tax In MI only; If tax exempt, please enter #.			
Total			

School or Organization Name:			
Name of Person Placing Order:		Job Title:	
Address:			
City:	State:	Zip:	Telephone:
Email:		Country:	
Purchase Order #:	OR	Master Card ☐	Visa ☐
Credit Card #:		Expiration: ___/20___	
Name on Card:		3-Digit Verification Code:	

BONUS OFFERS: **FREE Curriculum Supplements** with a purchase of $1000 or more. **FREE training video** (a $299.00 value) with purchase of $1500 or more. If your order qualifies for this offer, simply mark the video of your choice on the order form and write "free" in the total price column. (Curriculum Supplements will be sent automatically.)

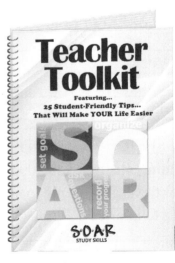